Jazzy Jars

Villa Biscotti

Mediterranean Vinaigrette

1 tablespoon Mediterranean Herb Ble...
1/4 cup olive oil
Juice of one lemon
1 tablespoon sugar

Mix all the ingredients and refrigerate for a few hours t...
the flavors to blend. Mix well before pouring onto mixed... vegetables.

Jazzy Jars

Marie Browning

Sterling Publishing Co., Inc.
New York

Prolific Impressions Production Staff

Editor in Chief: Mickey Baskett
Copy Editor: Phyllis Mueller
Graphics: Dianne Miller, Karen Turpin
Styling: Kirsten Jones
Photography: Jerry Mucklow
Administration: Jim Baskett

Library of Congress Cataloging-in-Publication Data Available

10 9 8 7 6 5 4

First paperback edition published in 2003 by
Sterling Publishing Co., Inc.
387 Park Avenue South, New York, NY 10016

© 2002 by Prolific Impressions, Inc.

Distributed in Canada by Sterling Publishing
C/o Canadian Manda Group, 165 Dufferin Street
Toronto, Ontario, Canada M6K 3H6
Distributed in the United Kingdom by GMC Distribution Services,
Castle Place, 166 High Street, Lewes, East Sussex, England BN7 1XU
Distributed in Australia by Capricorn Link (Australia) Pty. Ltd.
P.O. Box 704, Windsor, NSW 2756 Australia

Printed in China
All rights reserved

Sterling ISBN 0-8069-6873-7 Hardcover
　　　　　　1-4027-0858-0 Paperback

Acknowledgements

Marie Browning thanks the following manufacturers for their generous contribution of materials used in this book.

Alltrista Corporation
Indianapolis, IN 46250
www.alltrista.com
glass jars, canning jars, antique jar reproductions

American Art Clay Co., Inc.
Indianapolis, IN 46222
www.amaco.com
Fimo polymer clay, metal sheeting

Boutique Trims
South Lyon, MI 48178
www.boutiquetrims.com
metal charms

Delta Technical Coatings, Inc.
Whittier, CA 90601
www.deltacrafts.com
opaque and transparent PermEnamel paints for glass, stencils

Environmental Technologies
Fields Landing, CA 95537
www.eti-use.com
Envirotex Lite (two-part resin coating), AromaGel, (water-based gel air freshener), colorants, fragrances, jars and perforated lids, rub-on transfers

Heart & Home Collectibles, Inc.
Pickering, Ontario, Canada L1W 3V4
www.heartandhome.com
vintage peel-and-stick labels, jar lamp kits

Hunt Corporation
Philadelphia, PA 19103
www.hunt-corp.com
Painters opaque paint markers

Plaid Enterprises
Norcross, GA 30091
www.plaidonline.com
Apple Barrel Acrylic Gloss Paint, Royal Coat decoupage medium, Gallery Glass transparent glass paint and liquid leading, paint for plastic, fabric paints, All Night Media rubber stamps, stencils

San Francisco Herbs Co.
San Francisco, CA 94103
www.sfherb.com
potpourri and culinary dried botanicals

Xyron, Inc.
Scottsdale, AZ 85260
www.xyron.com
laminating and adhesive machine

About the Author
MARIE BROWNING

Marie Browning is a consummate craft designer who has made a career of designing products, writing books and articles, and teaching and demonstrating. You may have been charmed by her creative acumen but not been aware of the woman behind it; she has designed stencils, stamps, transfers, and a variety of other products for art and craft supply companies.

She is the author of three books on soapmaking: *300 Soap Recipes* (Sterling 2002), *Beautiful Handmade Natural Soaps* (Sterling, 1998) and *Melt & Pour Soapmaking* (Sterling, 2000). In addition to books about soapmaking, Browning has authored three other books published by Sterling: *Handcrafted Journals, Albums, Scrapbooks & More* (1999), *Making Glorious Gifts from Your Garden* (1999), and *Memory Gifts* (2000). Her articles and designs have appeared in *Handcraft Illustrated, Better Homes & Gardens, Canadian Stamper, Great American Crafts, All American Crafts,* and in numerous project books published by Plaid Enterprises, Inc.

Marie Browning earned a Fine Arts Diploma from Camosun College and attended the University of Victoria. She is a Certified Professional Demonstrator, a professional affiliate of the Canadian Craft and Hobby Association, and a member of the Stencil Artisans League and the Society of Craft Designers.

She lives, gardens, and crafts on Vancouver Island in Canada. She and her husband Scott have three children: Katelyn, Lena, and Jonathan. ❑

Marie's website: www.mariebrowning.com

CONTENTS

Gifts made with love delight the recipient and reward the giver. They are much more than handmade jars of culinary treats, fragrant offerings, and practical gifts – they are gifts of your time, thoughts, and creativity. When handmade gifts are packaged in decorated jars, the containers also become gifts that can be used for storage, as a lamp base, or as a decorative accessory. Celebrate your creativity with special gifts that express you. Don't make "I'm too busy" your motto; instead, slow down and make something unique and personal. Make everyday happenings a reason to give a gift in a jar: welcome to the neighborhood, thanks for dinner, congratulations on your retirement. Enter the exciting world of creating and the thrill of giving of one's self.

Create heartwarming gifts by decorating plain jars, then filling them with gifts of love. ❧

In this book, not only will you get ideas for filling the jars with culinary delights, fragrant potions, and other offerings; but you will learn creative ways to decorate the jars. Techniques such as decoupage, painting, stenciling, and embellishing with notions will make your jars look special. I will show you exciting ways to finish the lids, then make clever gift cards to go with them.

Plan to match gifts and jar decorations to the person; for example, while one person would enjoy relaxing bath salts, another would love a jar of homemade snacks. Make each decorated jar a most personal greeting and a wonderful expression of you. In this book, I've included projects that make perfect holiday gifts for festive winter celebrations, but many of the projects are great for giving all year long. Some of the projects require planning ahead; others are quick and easy.

Gifts that are made with the hands and given from the heart are always appreciated and treasured. The cliche, "It's the thought that counts" is true! Most of all, have fun!

CANNING JARS
Yesterday and Today

The process of applying heat to kill bacteria and removing oxygen from jars to prevent the food from deteriorating was invented in France in 1795 by Nicholas Appert. Appert, a chef, was determined to win the prize of 12,000 francs offered by Napoleon for a way to prevent military food supplies from spoiling. The first process involved garden peas preserved in champagne bottles. It was a French military secret but soon was leaked to the English. By 1810 an Englishman, Peter Durance, had patented the use of metal containers for canning and was opening factories. By the 1860s, canned foods were commonplace.

The major companies that manufacture canning jars today – Ball, Mason, and Kerr – were all started at least 100 years ago. The Ball brothers, Frank and Edmund, founded the Ball Corporation in 1880. They started with a wood-jacketed tin container for paint and varnish and soon expanded into the home-canning field. Ball still produces glass canning jars as well as space systems and electro-optic materials.

Jars used for home canning are often referred to as "Mason" jars after John L. Mason, inventor of the first common canning jar. Mason's patent expired in 1875. Since then, all canning jars are generally called mason jars. The first mason jars were made of blue-green glass. The originals are collectible and quite valuable.

The Kerr Company, founded in 1902, developed the two-piece lid, which is comprised of a flat seal and a separate screw-on band.

Types of Jars Available Today

Mason-style Canning Jars: Mason jars are glass jars available in half-pint, pint, quart, and half gallon sizes with standard or wide mouth openings. (The opening is called the "mouth" of the jar.) The glass of the jar may be molded or embossed with fruit motifs, diamond patterns, or company names and crests. Generally, I used less elaborate jars for the projects in this book, but fancier embossed jars can be substituted.

Plastic Storage Jars: Clear plastic storage jars with screw-on lids are useful when a glass jar is not practical, such as for gifts for children or for a gift that will be shipped. Plastic jars are sold as storage jars at packaging stores, container stores, and kitchen shops.

Old-fashioned Wire Bail Jars: These jars, with glass lids that are held in place with a wire clamp, are among my favorites. They cost a little more but give the finished project a nice appearance. Made in many sizes and shapes, they can be found at quality kitchen stores and department stores.

Decorative Jars: Many sizes, styles, and shapes of decorative jars are available – the selection is endless. Look for seasonal shaped candy and cookie jars, interesting shapes, and different colors of glass. I found these types of jars at crafts, kitchen supply, and gift stores.

Recycled Jars: Many jars can be recycled and used again for gift giving – just carefully soak the jars to remove labels and clean them thoroughly. You can save jars all year and be ready with a nice selection whenever you wish to create a gift. Lids with printing can be covered with spray paint, metal paints, or fabric tops. Recycled jars **should not** be used for canning foods.

Antique Jars: Antique glass jars are beautiful but their glass is more brittle so they are easier to break. If you use older jars, be sure they are free of chips and imperfections. If you are not sure of the value of an old jar, it may be wiser not to use it. One option is to seek out reproductions, so a vintage jar need not be used. (The price of some antique jars is amazing; some early colored-glass canning jars have been priced at up to $1,000 each!)

Jar Lid Possibilities

Typical **canning jar lids** come in two parts – a flat metal seal and a screw-on band. Some older jars have metal screw-on bands and flat glass tops. Still others have glass-lined zinc lids. If your neighbors or family members did a lot of home canning, chances are they saved jars from past generations – and many of these old jars make terrific containers. However, if you're planning to can food in jars, it's best to **always use** new jars and new seals.

There is a wide variety of **other types of lids** available for jars.

- Plastic screw-top lids are generally used for storage jars.
- One-piece metal screw-top lids (generally used by food manufacturers) can be reused when a seal is not required.
- Glass tops with bail-wire clamps (some with rubber gaskets) make attractive coverings.
- Wooden stoppers with rubber seals are a nice surface for decorating.
- Natural corks are another attractive way to secure the contents of a jar.
- Perforated metal lids for fragrance gifts are available in crafts shops or you can make your own.

Jars are an excellent base for a candle or lamp – check out your local craft outlet for lamp fixtures that screw right on canning jars in place of the lid.

You can also find **lid lamp kits** for canning jars that allow you to use a decorated jar as an oil lamp. The screw-on lid has a hole; a glass vial fits into the lid and a stopper placed on the vial holds a wick. The glass vial can be filled with lamp oil.

Glass **votive candle holders** – especially the clear glass ones shaped like flower pots – fit nicely in the tops of quart-size canning jars that contain layered potpourri or other decorative items.

For safety's sake, always give instructions for the use of your lighted jar gift and remind the recipient to never leave a burning candle unattended.

Cleaning Your Jars

Clean jars well inside and out before using or storing. You may need to soak the jars in hot soapy water to remove labels or price tags; remove the sticky residue left by stickers with a product designed for that purpose. When you're ready to use the jar, rub the outside with a soft, lint-free rag and rubbing alcohol to remove all surface grease and fingerprints. Follow the directions for sterilizing and cleaning jars for food in the Culinary Gifts section.

PAINTED JARS

There are a variety of painting techniques and types of paints that can be used to beautify your jars. This chapter will show examples of the range of products available to create the look you desire.

With a variety of techniques from primitive painting and simple stenciling to the look of stained glass, you will learn how to paint on glass or plastic jars. The twelve projects that follow will delight you with painted pleasure.

Choosing the Right Paint

Even though it seems quite simple, the question I'm most often asked when I teach is, "What paint do I use on this surface?" Here's the rule: Always select a paint intended for use on the surface you are decorating. Read the label on the paint container to determine the paint's compatibility with your surface. This rule goes for painting on glass or on metal lids or a plastic jar.

You can use acrylic craft paints for painting on untreated glass, but the paint will rub off when handled and not be permanent. If you "rough up" a glass surface with a coat of matte spray, you can use acrylic paint, but the surface won't be washable. However, if you use acrylic glass paint, your design will be permanent and will not chip or wash off when fully cured. On the following page you will find information about the types of paints you can use on glass.

> **TIPS**
>
> • **Working on the jar.** To hold the jar while decorating and painting, place your hand inside to keep fingerprints off and the paint from smudging. I like to fold an old towel and place it on my work surface to create a "cradle" to hold the jar steady while I work. I also like to place a clean sheet of white paper in clear glass jars while I decorate them – it helps me see my work-in-process.
>
> • **Allow enough time.** Decorate the jar and allow the paint and glue to cure fully before adding the contents.
>
> • **Provide instructions for care.** If your finished decorated jar needs any special care, write down the instructions and give them to the recipient with the gift.

Pictured at right: Primitive Striped Jars. See instructions for these jars on page 19.

Today we are fortunate to be able to choose from several varieties of paints suitable for painting on glass. They offer transparent or opaque coverage and come in a wide range of colors. Many manufacturers have recognized the popularity of painting on glass and have developed paints specifically for that purpose. Check out your local craft shop when choosing a paint.

Painting Supplies

■ TRANSPARENT GLASS PAINTS

These are transparent paints that are often used to resemble stained glass. For best results when applying the paint, squeeze it from the bottle directly onto the surface of the jar. In some cases it can be brushed onto the surface. These paints often come with a liquid "leading" or outline paint that is applied before filling in with the transparent colors to create the faux glass stain technique. These types of paints **are not washable** so should be used for decorative purposes only such as for candle jars. This type of paint is not recommended to use with culinary products.

Check label to see if the paint is water-based paint. Choosing a water-based variety will make cleanup much easier.

■ ACRYLIC HIGH GLOSS PAINTS

These paints are durable, opaque, high gloss acrylic paints for glass and offer a wide variety of pre-mixed colors in convenient squeeze bottles. Do not thin paints with water – if you need them thinned, use blending mediums or thinning mediums manufactured for that brand of paint. While still wet, the paints clean up easily with soap and water. These types of paints are great to use with culinary products.

These types of paints can be baked in a home oven to make them more durable and washable. (Check labels to see if this is possible with the paint you have chosen.) To bake, let paint dry a full 48 hours. Place the glass jar in a conventional oven (not pre-heated) and heat to 325 degrees. Bake for 10 minutes. Turn off the oven and allow jar to cool in oven before removing. After baking, painted jars can be hand washed. Washing in the dishwasher is **not** recommended.

Painting with acrylic high gloss paints

■ AIR-DRY ENAMEL PAINTS FOR GLASS

There are some brands of opaque, brush-on glass paint available that air-dry to a high-gloss, waterproof finish. Choose a brand that is water-based acrylic and non-toxic. Water-based types can be cleaned-up with soap and water. Recommended for use with culinary products.

■ PAINTS FOR PLASTIC

These brush-on paints are especially formulated for adhering to plastic and drying to a durable, waterproof finish. I have used these on the plastic jars shown in this book. I like to use the water-based type so that brushes and spills can be easily cleaned up with soap and water.

■ PAINT PENS

A colorful selection of paint pens are available in craft shops. They are great for detailing and for simple jar decoration without the fuss of paints and brushes. Paint pens come in many colors and in fine, medium, and calligraphy chisel point tips.

■ FABRIC PAINTS

The dimensional type that squeeze directly from the bottle to the surface and the brush-on type are both great for using on glass jars. The dimensional type is especially effective for special effects like wording or facial features. And they are so easy to use – like holding a pen. ⟶

■ ACRYLIC CRAFT PAINTS

These are the types of paints most often used on wood. However, some brands have a **glass medium** that can be applied to the glass to prepare it for the paint. The medium can be used over the dried paint to seal it. You could also use a matte acrylic spray as a primer and sealer. These paints are not washable or very durable on glass. Even when sealed, the paint can easily be scraped from the jar. They are not recommended to use with culinary products.

■ PAINT APPLICATORS

You will need a variety of good quality **artist's brushes**. These are the ones I used:

• 1/2" and 1" flat glaze brushes, for basecoating and painting large motifs

• #1 and #4 round brushes, for general painting and details
• #0 and #00 liners, for fine detailing
   A variety of **sponges** can also be used to apply paint:
• Fine textured sea sponges, for basecoating and sponged finishes
• Dense foam sponges (the type used for applying make-up), for stenciling and edging

■ CHOOSING GLUES

For gluing items to jars, I find **silicone-based glue for glass** works best. It also works well for gluing wood to glass, metal to glass, or plastic to glass. I also use this type of glue for attaching items to metal or wooden lids. Silicone-based glue takes a bit of time to dry, and you'll need to prop the jar so it lies horizontally while the glue dries.

A **glue gun** can be used for attaching light objects, such as a ribbon, to the jar for an instant hold. **White craft glue** is used for gluing unbaked polymer clay pieces to a jar or lid before baking in the oven.

■ OTHER SUPPLIES

• **Paper towels** for cleanup
• **Water basin** for rinsing and cleaning brushes
• **Low-tack masking tape** (often called "painter's tape")for taping patterns if patterns are placed inside of jar.
• **Transfer paper and a stylus** if patterns are to be transferred to outside of jar.
• **Brush-cleaning soap** for brush cleaning and care.

PAINT CAUTIONS & TIPS

• Always follow the paint manufacturer's directions carefully. Do not assume all glass paints are the same. Some require a pre-conditioner or primer and a clear protective topcoat to be permanent.

• It is not a good idea to mix different manufacturers' products, e.g., don't use a paint color from Company A and a topcoat from Company B. Each company carefully formulates its paints, mediums, primers, and topcoats to work best together and cannot guarantee results when its products are used with other companies' products.

How to Paint on Jars

SURFACE PREPARATION

Jars should be clean and dry before paint is applied. Rub down the surface well with rubbing alcohol, holding the jar by the neck to avoid fingerprints. When using paints specifically manufactured for painting on glass, follow the paint manufacturer's directions carefully for preparing the glass surface. Some glass paints require an undercoat or primer. If recommended, be sure to use one.

TRANSFERRING DESIGNS

For transparent jars, place a photocopy of the pattern in the jar. Use a small piece of tape inside the jar to hold the pattern in place and put two or three crumpled paper towels in the jar to hold the pattern against the inside of the jar. (This is easier than taping all around the pattern to hold

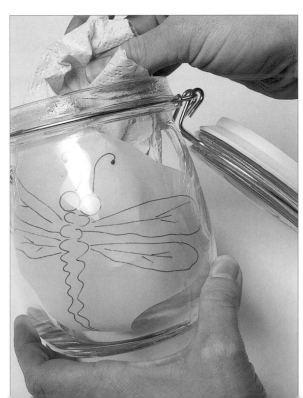

it flat against the glass.)

When transferring a pattern to painted glass, use wax-free transfer paper and choose a colored transfer paper, such as red or blue, which is easier to see on the glass surface. Carefully tape the transfer paper in place over the jar, making sure the paper is right side down. With a stylus, trace the pattern firmly to transfer the design to the jar. Placing a blank piece of white paper in the jar makes it easier to see the transferred design.

BASECOATING

For a full, opaque coverage, brush on the paint with a fairly heavy application, heavy enough so it coats the glass but not so heavy that the paint drips and sags. Two or three coats are usually needed; be sure to let the paint dry fully between coats.

Another method of basecoating is to apply the paint by stippling with a sea sponge. Make sure the sponge is damp and all excess water has been squeezed out. Dip the sponge into the paint and apply to the jar in an up and down dabbing motion. You will need to apply two or three coats and let each coat dry fully. This technique gives the surface a slight texture.

USING PAINT PENS

Paint pens come in many colors and in fine, medium, and calligraphy chisel-point tips. Use them to add accents and lettering to jars or for details and outlines. Be sure the paint is fully dry and cured before using a paint pen on it. Always test the pens on the bottom of the jar to make sure they are compatible with the glass paint used.

ANTIQUING WITH PAINT

Antiquing gives an aged look to projects, and it's easy to do with diluted paint. Use the same type of paint for antiquing that you used to paint a project. Here are some examples:
- **Over acrylic paint:** Thin dark brown acrylic paint with an acrylic varnish or acrylic paint extender. Brush the mixture over the surface, then wipe with a soft rag.
- **Over glass paint:** Thin glass paint with a glass paint varnish. Brush over the project, then wipe with a soft rag.

CREATING FAUX ETCHED GLASS

The look of etched glass can be created with frosted white acrylic glass paint and a dense foam sponge. Using paint is faster than chemical etching, and you don't have to use any harsh chemicals. Using stencils to apply the designs is my favorite method of adding a subtle glass etched look. These jars are examples of faux etched glass: French Country Air Jar, Joyful Scents Jar, Beachfront Property Lamp Jar, and Faux Etched Glass Tea Jar.

STENCILING

    You can stencil designs using a pre-cut purchased stencil or a design you cut yourself on freezer paper. The photo shows a variety of pre-cut types to use.

Photo 1

Photo 2

Photo 3

1. Photocopy the pattern and tape the copy on a piece of freezer paper that is shiny side up and 1" larger all around than the pattern.

2. Place the papers on a cutting mat and cut out the motifs with a sharp craft knife.

3. Spray the backside of the stencil with a coat of spray adhesive. (This makes your stencil adhere to the jar and allows you to remove it without tearing.) **See Photo 1.**

4. Let the adhesive dry for 10 minutes and position the stencil on the jar.

5. Place a puddle of paint onto a palette or a disposable plate. Load a make-up sponge with paint by dabbing it into the puddle of paint. **See Photo 2.**

6. Press or dab the sponge on paper towels to remove excess paint. **See Photo 3.** The key here is to **use very little paint**. Glass is not forgiving; even a little too much paint can seep under the stencil, so it's better to use very little paint and apply as many coats as necessary to achieve the effect you want.

7. Stipple the color into the open areas of the stencil with an up and down dabbing motion. **See Photo 4.** *Note: The circular, swirling method of stenciling does not work on the slick glass surface.*

Photo 4

These striped jars are easy and quick to paint and would make nice accents to a country kitchen. For a simple but striking flower arrangement, remove the flat glass lid inserts, replace the bands, and fill the jars with garden-fresh daisies.

Primitive Striped Jars

pictured on page 13

JAR TYPE
Three quart-size canning jars with screw-on bands and flat glass lids

PAINT TYPE
Air-dry enamel paints for glass

JAR DECORATION
1. Using a 1/2" flat brush, paint stripes on each jar, one color at a time. Let each color dry before adding the next color. One jar is painted with blue and white stripes, another with red and white stripes, and the third with blue, red, and white stripes.
2. To make the jars look old, antique with a mixture of equal amounts of glass paint varnish and dark brown acrylic enamel glass paint.
3. Using an old toothbrush, spatter the jars with the antiquing mixture.

LID DECORATION
Prime the metal bands, then paint with an "instant rust" paint kit.

EMBELLISHMENTS
Wrap 20" of 20 gauge black wire around the neck of each jar. Attach three rusty metal stars (cut from sheet metal and painted with the same paint you used to paint the bands) to the ends of the wire. ❑

Another simple idea for a painted jar – use these for storage and to add bright accents to a room.

It's a quick and easy project you can do in an afternoon or on the spur of the moment.

Whimsical Blossoms Jars

JAR TYPE
Two quart-size and one pint-size canning jars with screw-on bands and flat metal seals

PAINT TYPE
Air-dry enamel paints for glass

JAR DECORATION - YELLOW QUART JAR
1. Paint a 1-1/2" wide yellow band around the bottom of the jar and a 2" wide yellow band around the top. Let dry completely.
2. Add white dots (for the flower centers) at the painted edge by dipping the handle end of a paintbrush in a puddle of paint and dotting on the jar.
3. With a #4 round brush add blue flower petals and green leaves.

JAR DECORATION - BLUE QUART JAR
1. Paint a 1-1/2" wide blue band around the bottom of the jar and a 2" wide blue band around the top. Let dry completely.
2. Add white dots (for the flower centers) at the painted edge by dipping the handle end of a paintbrush in a puddle of paint and dotting on the jar.
3. With a #4 round brush add yellow flower petals and green leaves.

JAR DECORATION - PINT JAR
1. Paint a 2" wide blue band around the middle of the jar. Let dry completely.
2. Add white dots (for the flower centers) by dipping the handle end of a paintbrush in a puddle of paint and dotting on the jar.
3. With a #4 round brush add yellow flower petals and green leaves.

LID DECORATION
Spray the flat metal seals with glossy white metal spray paint.

EMBELLISHMENTS
1. Add loopy bows of narrow satin ribbon to the necks of the jars.
2. Glue daisy buttons on the bows on the quart jars and a small puffy gingham heart on the bow on the pint jar. ❏

These jars are easy for the novice painter – the details are added with paint pens. A painting worksheet is included on the following pages along with a pattern for the design.

Countryside Jars

JAR TYPE

Three pint-sized canning jars with screw-on bands and flat glass lids.

PAINT TYPE

Air-dry enamel paint or acrylic gloss paint.
Paint pens

JAR DECORATION

1. Trace or copy pattern and tape to the inside of the jar. *See following pages for patterns for jars.*

2. Starting at the top of the jar, double load a 1" flat brush and paint the colored bands. Let dry and repeat to add a second coat. Refer to the patterns for color suggestions.

3. Use paint pens to add outlines and details.
See following page for a painted example of the design on jars.

LID DECORATION

Spray paint the screw-on lid with glossy white metal spray paint. ❑

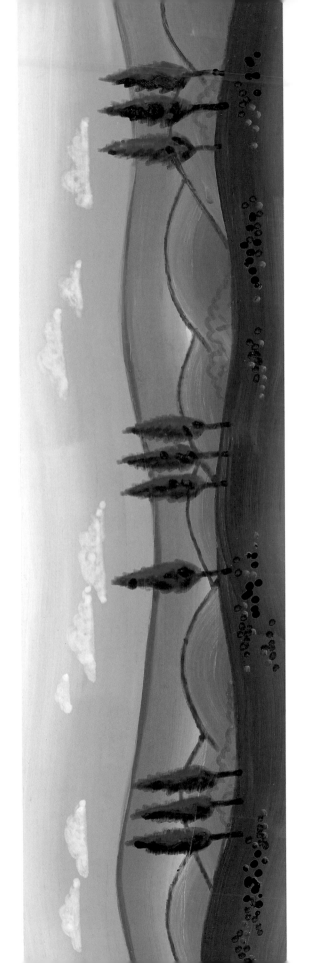

PATTERNS: *Enlarge @118% for actual size*

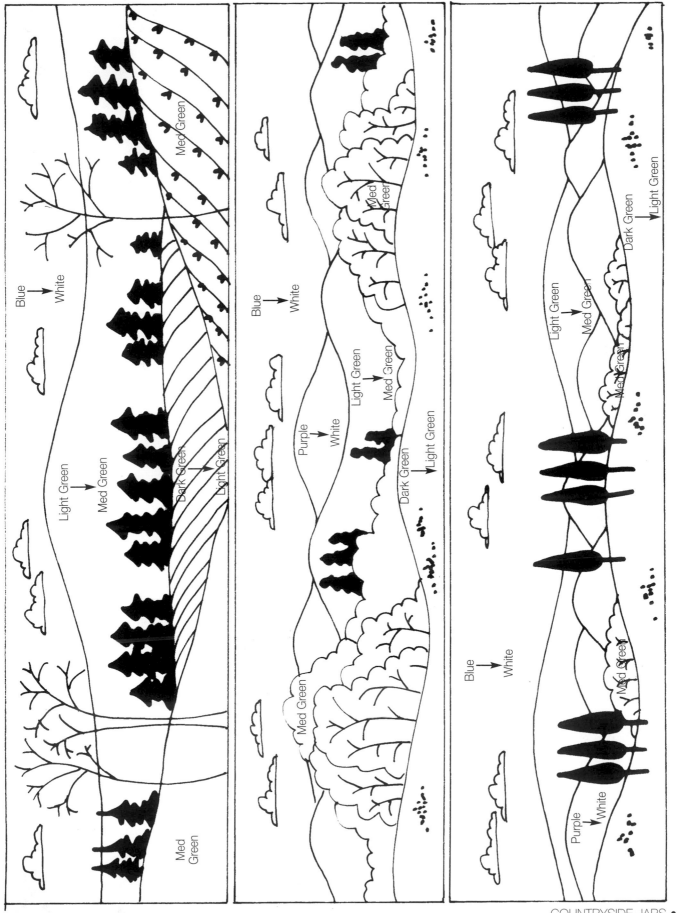

These stenciled jars make colorful kitchen accents and are perfect for storing a variety of food items.

To make it easy, we've included patterns to cut your own stencil for the design and a color example of the stenciling.

Stenciled Fruit Jars

JAR TYPE
Two quart-size canning jars with screw-on bands and glass lids

JAR DECORATION

1. Base paint the jars with an opaque coverage of acrylic gloss paint using tan and antique white paint. Stipple the paint onto the jars with a sea sponge. Pick up the colors on the sponge and stipple randomly, blending one color into the other. Two coats are needed. Let dry completely.

2. Cut a stencil from freezer paper or brown paper using the patterns provided or buy a fruit stencil. Spray the back of the stencil with spray adhesive.

Below: Stencils cut from freezer paper

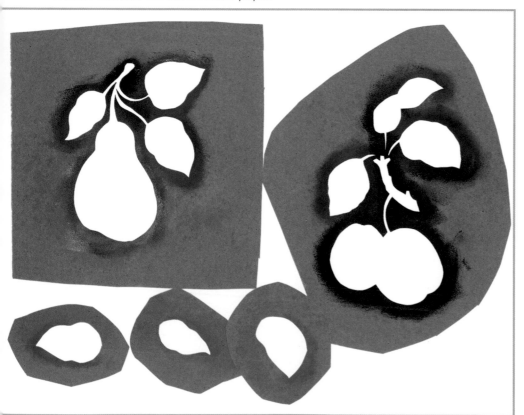

COLOR PALETTE
Acrylic gloss paints
Plum Jar:
Real Yellow
Mossy Green
Forest Green
Rose Wine
Cranberry Red
Coffee Bean

Pear Jar:
Real Yellow
Terra Cotta
Rose Wine
Coffee Bean
Mossy Green
Forest Green

3. Stencil plums:
   - Stencil the center highlight area of the plums and the leaves with Real Yellow.
   - Stencil the plums with Rose Wine, being careful not to paint over the yellow highlighted area in the center.
   - Shade around the edge of the plums with Cranberry Red.
   - Stencil the leaves with Mossy Green, being careful not to paint over the yellow highlighted area.

Continued on page 28

continued from page 26

- Shade the edges of the leaves with Forest Green and Coffee Bean.
- Stencil stem with Coffee Bean.
- Stencil shadow leaves with Mossy Green.

4. Stencil pears:
   - Stencil the center highlight area of the pears and leaves with Real Yellow.
   - Add a blush to the pears with Rose Wine.
   - Shadow around the edge of pears with Terra Cotta.

- Stencil the leaves with Mossy Green, being careful not to paint over the yellow highlighted area.
- Shade the edges of the leaves with Forest Green and Coffee Bean.
- Stencil stem with Coffee Bean
- Stencil shadow leaves with Mossy Green.

5. Paint the details with a #0 liner brush using Coffee Bean.

6. Spatter the jar with Coffee Bean using an old toothbrush for spattering.

LID DECORATION

1. Paint the glass parts of the lids with the same tan and antique white paints used for the jars, using a sponge to stipple the colors. Let dry.

2. Apply an antiquing wash to the metal bands by brushing on a coat of brown metal paint and wiping off the excess.

EMBELLISHMENTS

Tie raffia bows around the necks of the jars. ❑

PAINTING EXAMPLE

Stencil plums and leaves

Add stenciled shadow leaves and liner brush details.

Plums

Extra Leaves

Pears

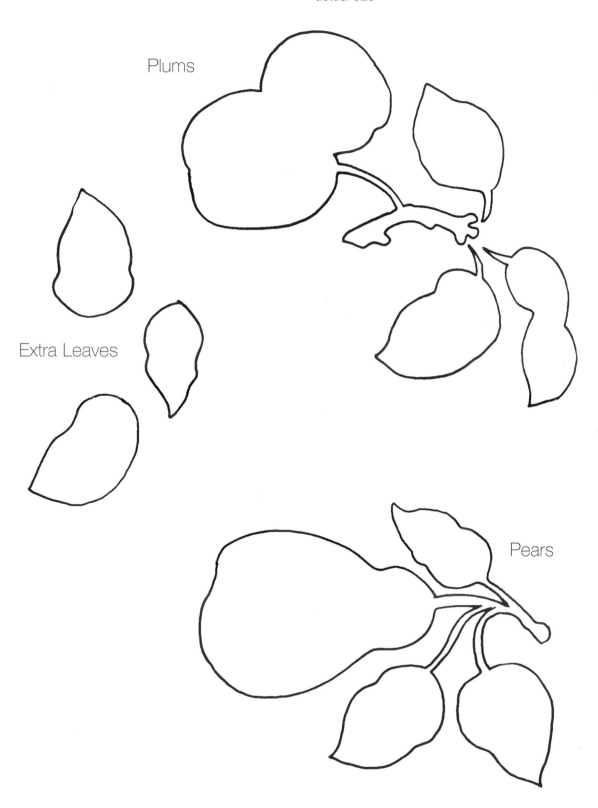

Decoupage and painting have been combined on these jars to create canisters that make great kitchen containers or proud vessels for homemade drink mixes. The vintage-inspired labels were computer generated, then painted with botanical accents of coffee and tea plants. If you cannot find old jars, use reproductions.

Tea & Coffee Canisters

COLOR PALETTE

Acrylic gloss paint
for tea:
Patina Green
Forest Green
White
Antique White
Pink Blush
Coffee Bean

for coffee:
Mossy Green
Forest Green
Rose Wine
Coffee Bean

JAR TYPE

Two quart-size old-fashioned canning jars with glass lids and wire bails

JAR DECORATION

1. Create your own 3-1/2" x 5" labels on a computer or use the ones printed on page 32. You may make a color copy of the labels to cutout and decoupage to your jar. *Option:* Hand letter or stencil letters with a purchased alphabet stencil.

2. Give an aged appearance to the labels by spattering with brown acrylic paint thinned with water and using an old toothbrush for spattering.

3. Lightly sponge the edges using a dense foam sponge and the spattering mixture.

4. Affix the labels to the jars with decoupage medium. Let dry.

5. Trace the coffee bean patterns provided on the following pages and transfer to jar using transfer paper and a stylus.

6. Paint the designs. Let dry.

EMBELLISHMENTS

1. Tie sheer ribbons around the necks of the jars.

2. To the coffee canister, add a painted wooden scoop. Accent the scoop with a metal charm. Attach a small hook to loop on the ribbon. To the tea canister, add a metal tea ball. ❑

Tea & Coffee Canister Labels

ORANGE PEKOE

TEA

Premium Ceylon Tea

DARK ROASTED

COFFEE

Premium Blend

PAINTING PATTERNS
actual size

Tea

Coffee

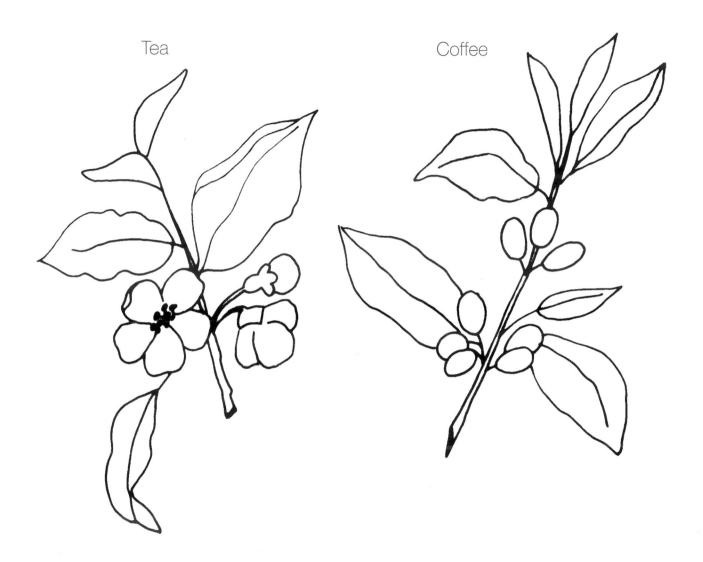

This jar is filled with magic tricks. Directions for the tricks are wrapped in a 5" x 7" piece of decorative paper with "SECRET MAGIC WORDS ENCLOSED" written on the label. Many toy collections can be packaged this way, providing a wonderful presentation as well as a handy storage container.

The Magic Jar

Painting on Plastic Jars

Plastic jars are a wise choice for decorating when giving a gift to a child – you can collect a selection by recycling food containers. Paints specifically designed for plastic cover containers in two coats to create an opaque surface.

I also enjoy using fabric paints, which come in handy squeeze bottles and tubes, for painting plastic surfaces. When completely dry and cured, they are remarkably strong and durable. Fabric paints are easy enough for children to use, so you can let the kids help decorate jars.

JAR TYPE
Gallon-size plastic jar with white metal screw-on lid

PAINT TYPE
Paint for plastic
Dimensional fabric paint

JAR DECORATION
1. Tape off a 2-1/2" band around the middle of the jar with masking tape. Sponge the band with blue plastic paint. Let dry. Remove tape.
2. Write "Abracadabra" on the painted blue band with blue fabric paint. Immediately, while the paint is still wet, sprinkle tiny star sequins and clear, hole-less beads on the wet paint. Let dry completely.
3. Glue large multi-colored star sequins on and around the band.

LID DECORATION
1. Make a label by cutting out a paper circle from gold metallic paper with decorative edge scissors to fit the top of the lid.
2. Cut a star from blue paper. Punch with a star-shaped hole punch to accent.
3. Write the words "My Magic Kit" on the star with a gold paint pen.

EMBELLISHMENTS
1. Wrap a yard of gold star garland around the magic tricks on the inside for extra sparkle.
2. Wrap another yard of gold star garland around the neck of the jar. ❏

Pictured at right: Magic Jar and Jar of Fun. Instructions for the "Jar of Fun" are on the following page.

This is a wonderful gift to keep a child busy on a rainy day! It's also fun to give to adults as an "Executive Stress Reliever" – decorate the jar with black paper and gold lettering to fit in an office. This would also be a hit for a craft bazaar.

Jar of Fun

pictured on page 35

Contents: Smelly, Sparkly Play Dough in three colors, each wrapped in plastic food wrap (Recipe included.)

JAR TYPE

Small plastic storage jar with white metal screw-on lid

PAINT TYPE

Fabric paint

JAR DECORATION

1. Cut a 3" wide strip of yellow paper long enough to wrap around the jar. Cover with sticky-back clear plastic laminate. (This gives the paper a more durable finish and a shiny look.)
2. Make a child-type drawing on the paper with fabric paint. (Let the kids help out.) Write the recipient's name on the label. Let dry completely. Attach paper to the jar.

RECIPE

Smelly, Sparkly Play Dough

1 cup flour
1/2 cup salt
2 teaspoons cream of tartar
1 cup water
1 tablespoon cooking oil
Unsweetened drink mix (three flavors for three different colors)
1 tablespoon Iridescent glitter

Combine flour, salt, and cream of tartar in saucepan. Stir in water and cooking oil. Heat, stirring, until very thick and hard to stir. (The mixture will resemble mashed potatoes). Remove from heat. Let cool 5 minutes.

Turn out on a lightly floured surface. Divide in 3 equal parts. Add 1 teaspoon unsweetened drink mix and 1 teaspoon iridescent glitter to each part. Knead until pliable and an even color. Wrap in plastic wrap to keep fresh. Store in an airtight plastic container. ❏

LID DECORATION

Write "MY JAR OF FUN" on the top of the jar with fabric paint. Accent the letters with dots of paint in a contrasting color.

EMBELLISHMENTS

1. Tie a bow of sheer pink ribbon around the neck of the jar.
2. To make the gift tag, cut a 3" x 6" piece of folded card stock. Layer on three squares of decorative paper (2-1/2", 2", 1-1/2"). Remove the shank from an umbrella button. Glue button onto center panel. Write "Rainy Day Fun" on the tag. ❏

This would be a great "Welcome, autumn" gift filled with homemade candied pretzels or spiced nuts.

Pumpkin Candy Jar

JAR TYPE

Decorative glass pumpkin jar

PAINT TYPE

Acrylic gloss paints

JAR & LID DECORATION

1. Paint jar and lid with two coats of rust paint, using a sea sponge.
2. Paint the stem with green.
3. Lightly sponge green paint on the jar to add interest, blending it in with another soft coat of rust paint, if necessary.
4. Paint the face with black, using a #4 round brush.

EMBELLISHMENTS

1. Trace the leaf patterns. Place a sheet of 30 gauge copper on a soft surface, such as a piece of foam sheeting or a carpet sample. Place the leaf tracings on the copper. Go over the lines of the leaves with a ballpoint pen to emboss.
2. Cut out the leaves using heavy duty scissors.
3. Sponge lightly with metal paints for an aged look. Let dry.
4. Using an awl, make a hole at the base of each leaf. Cut two 20" pieces of 26 gauge green wire. Wrap the wire around the neck of the jar and attach the leaves. Coil the ends of the wire for a decorative finish. ❏

LEAF PATTERNS – *Enlarge @175% for actual size.*

Transparent acrylic paints can be used to create a stained glass effect on glass surfaces. The paints are packaged in handy squeeze tubes for easy application. The paint is squeezed directly from the bottle onto the jar surface. To paint the lead lines of the designs, use gold, black, or silver dimensional paint or use simulated leading adhesive strips.

Stained Glass Floral Jars

When designing on the three-dimensional surface of a jar, it is best to divide the area into panels with leading paint or strips. Work on one panel at a time, letting it dry completely before proceeding to the next. This prevents you from accidentally smudging wet paint while you work and allows the jars to dry horizontally, preventing drips.

Calla Lily Jar & Lily of the Valley Jar

COLOR PALETTE

Transparent paint for glass
for Calla Lily:
White Pearl
Ruby Red
Ivy Green
Celadon Green
Emerald Green
Clear (for background)

for Lily of the Valley:
White Pearl
Ruby Red
Ivy Green
Celadon Green
Emerald Green
Clear (for background)

Calla Lily jar is pictured on page 39.
Lily of the Valley jar is pictured on page 41.

These two jars are decorated the same way, using different patterns for the designs. The transparent glass paint used around the design gives the look of hand-blown glass. See pages that follow for patterns and color recommendations.

JAR TYPE

Two quart-size glass jars with two-piece lids (screw-on bands and flat metal seals)

SIMULATED LEAD STRIPS

Gold for the jar divisions *Note: you can purchase pre-made lead strips or you can make your own by squeezing out the simulated liquid lead onto a sheet of clear cling-free plastic. The strips will dry and can be removed from the plastic and applied to the jar. See photo 1 showing making of the leading strips.*

SIMULATED LIQUID LEAD

Gold for outline of design.

Continued on page 40

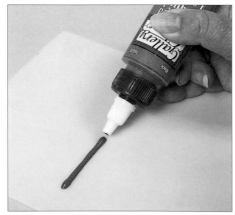

Photo 1

continued from page 38

JAR DECORATION

1. Divide jar into four panels with gold leading strips. See diagram for the divisions. See photo 2 showing placing the leading strips.
2. Finish all joints with gold liquid lead.
3. Place pattern inside jar and trace design with gold liquid lead. Do one panel at a time, letting each dry completely before proceeding to the next one.
4. Paint design with colored glass paint. The paint squeezes directly from the bottle onto the surface of the jar. Use the nozzle to move the paint around to cover the surface. See photo 3.
5. After an area has been painted, it can be moved out or given texture by "combing" it with a toothpick. See photo 4.
6. Fill in around designs with clear transparent glass paint.

LID DECORATION

Paint metal seal with gold spray paint. ❑

at neck

1-1/2"

3" x 4-1/4" panel

3/4"

at corners

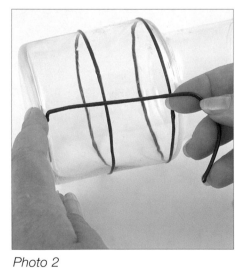

Photo 2

Photo 3

Photo 4

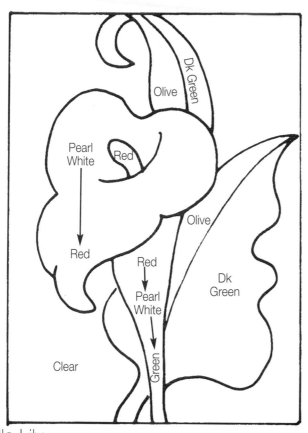

Calla Lily

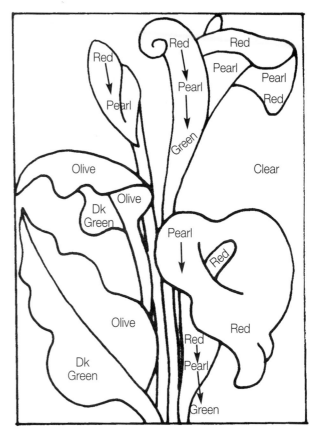

PATTERNS — ACTUAL SIZE

Lily of the Valley

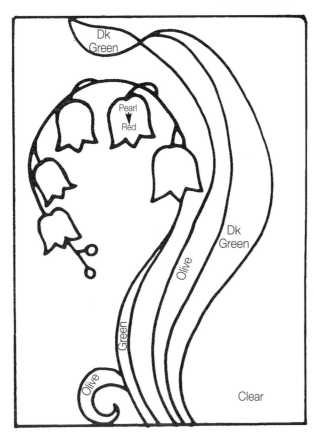

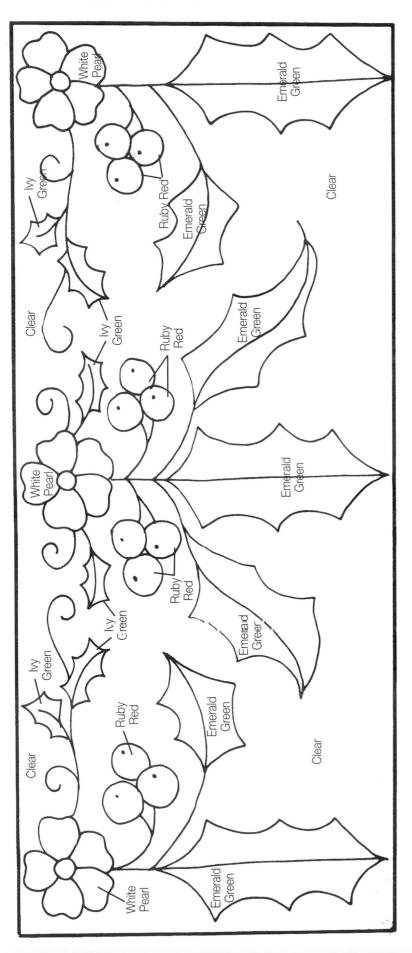

PATTERN

Light of My Life

Enlarge @115% for actual size

Instructions on page 44

This jar makes a lovely holiday decoration when outfitted with a lamp oil burner kit. A small vial holds the lamp oil. Iridescent excelsior is used to fill the jar.

Light of My Life

COLOR PALETTE

Transparent paint for glass
White Pearl (flower)
Emerald Green (holly)
Ivy Green (holly)
Ruby Red (berries)
Clear (background)

JAR TYPE
Quart-size canning jar with lamp kit for lid

SIMULATED LIQUID LEAD
Gold for outline of design.

JAR DECORATION
1. Trace or photo copy the pattern and tape it inside of the jar.

2. Place pattern inside jar and trace design with gold simulated liquid lead. Jar must be flat to outline the design with simulated liquid lead. Do one section at a time, allow to dry, then turn to continue outline design. Allow to dry.

3. Paint design with colored glass paint. The paint squeezes directly from the bottle onto the surface of the jar. Use the nozzle to move the paint around to cover the surface.

4. After an area has been painted, it can be moved out or given texture by "combing" it with a toothpick.

5. Fill in around designs with clear transparent glass paint.

LID DECORATION
1. Install lamp kit.

2. Glue gold ribbon around edge of lid. ❏

This pretty jar is filled with a fragrant air freshener gel that will scent and refresh a room for up to 60 days.

Floral Fragrance Jar

Contents: Gel fragrance tinted with blue color and scented with plumaria fragrance (See the Gifts of Scent section (page 112) for instructions on "Making Gel Air Fresheners.")

JAR TYPE

Small square jar (recycled) with gold perforated lid

SIMULATED LIQUID LEAD

Gold for outlining design and dividing the jar.

JAR DECORATION

Paint a faux stained glass flower design, using the pattern provided. See "Stained Glass Floral Jars" projects on previous pages for details on painting with transparent glass paint.

LID DECORATION

Punch ventilation holes in the lid, using an awl and hammer.

EMBELLISHMENTS

1. Tie a 12" piece of green ribbon around the neck of the jar.
2. Make a matching gift card by painting the flower design on a 4" x 5" piece of clear plastic sheet. Place in a window card with an oval opening. Write around opening with a gold gel pen. ❑

PATTERN FOR FLORAL FRAGRANCE JAR
actual size

Using decoupage allows you to decorate jars with many types of paper, including wrapping paper, printed napkins, stamped handmade papers, and postage stamps. The array of papers specifically designed for decoupage includes labels, floral designs, and vintage motifs.

DECOUPAGED JARS

SUPPLIES FOR DECOUPAGE

Paper decorations of your choice
Decoupage medium
Sponge brush for applying medium
Craft knife
Sharp scissors for cutting designs
Cutting mat
Freezer paper as working surface

Optional:
Thin-bodied white glue as an alternative to gluing paper to surface
Two-part resin coating as an alternative coating

Decoupage is done in three basic steps: cutting, gluing, and sealing. Neatly trimmed images and careful gluing will result in heirloom quality projects you will be proud to display and give as gifts. Additional coats of decoupage medium will seal the surface and protect the paper but won't be waterproof. If you wish the design to be waterproof and permanent, apply a two-part resin coating, following the instructions in the section titled "Making Resin-coated Jars & Lids."

The Basic Technique

CUTTING

1. Trim away excess paper from around the image you wish to cut out.
2. Use a craft knife and cutting board to cut out any areas inside the image before cutting around the outer edges.
3. Use small, sharp, pointed scissors to cut around the edge of the design. Hold scissors at a 45 degree angle so the paper is cut with a slightly beveled edge. (The beveled edge helps the image adhere snugly against the surface.) Move the paper – not the scissors – as you cut.

Options: After cutting out an image, decorate it further with stamping or antique the edges with an inkpad, using a dense foam sponge.

GLUING

1. Protect your work surface with freezer paper.
2. Using a foam brush, lightly coat the back of the image with decoupage medium. See photo 1.
3. Position the image on the surface and smooth it with your fingers, pushing out wrinkles and air bubbles. Allow to dry. See photo 2.

SEALING

1. Apply two to three coats of the decoupage medium with the foam brush to seal the paper. See photo 3. The finish appears cloudy when wet, but will dry crystal clear.
2. If you are planning to coat your project with pour-on resin, coat the decoupaged surface with thin-bodied white glue to seal. Let dry, then apply the resin.

ADDING A FINE CRACKLED FINISH

Kits are available for creating a fine crackled finish over decoupage to give the look of age and wear. Choose a varnish crackle kit (not an aged paint kit) – it usually includes a basecoat and a topcoat that both dry clear. The basecoat and topcoat dry at different rates and create the fine crackled effect.

The crackling is hard to see until it is antiqued. Use a white or light-hued antiquing medium over a dark image and a dark brown or black antiquing medium over a light image. Wipe the antiquing on the crackled surface with a soft rag and remove any excess.

Photo 1

Photo 2

Photo 3

A collage of layered papers and interesting postage stamps are decoupaged onto the jar with decoupage medium, then accented with gold leafing.

Paper Collage Jar

Examples of paper used to decoupage.

JAR TYPE

Pint-size caning jar with screw-on band and flat glass lid

PAPERS NEEDED

Layer 1 - Rice paper with gold filigree print.

Layer 2 - Artists' signatures torn from decoupage paper, edges rubbed with brown ink from an inkpad (use a make-up sponge to apply ink).

Layer 3 - Postage stamps and color photocopies of decorative paper seals.

JAR DECORATION

1. Glue on layers of paper, adhering them with decoupage medium.
2. Apply double-sided tape, 1/4" and 1/8" wide, around jar. Apply gold leaf to bands. See "How to Apply Metal Leafing."
3. Seal with a coat of decoupage finish. Let dry.
4. Antique with brick red paint. Let dry.
5. Apply a two-part resin coating to jar, following the instructions in the "Making Resin-coated Jars & Lids" section.

LID DECORATION

1. Gild the screw-on band with gold leaf.
2. Antique with brick red paint. Let dry.
3. Varnish to protect. ❑

A set of battery-powered tiny lights – reminiscent of fireflies – illuminates a scene inside a jar. Instead of a lid, a piece of floral foam holds the lights in place and an arrangement of silk greenery.

Peek-a-boo Forest
Floral Arrangement

JAR TYPE
Wide-mouth quart-size canning jar

OTHER SUPPLIES
Handmade paper
Rubber stamp with script writing
Rubber stamp with fern design
Rubber stamp with spatter design
Three colors of ink - green, brown, light brown

JAR DECORATION
Outside:
1. Stamp handmade paper with a script stamp, a fern stamp, and a spatter stamp.
2. Tear paper into 2" pieces.
3. Decoupage the pieces of paper to jar in an overlapping fashion, leaving an area in front of jar uncovered.
4. Wrap natural raffia around neck of jar.
5. Apply two coats of decoupage medium to the jar and the raffia lip.

Inside:
1. Mix aquarium gravel with two-part resin coating and spoon into jar. Be careful not to let resin drip on the inner sides of the jar.
2. Place a plastic frog and acorns or pine cones in jar. Arrange silk ferns and greenery in the back of the jar. The items will adhere to the resin finish on the gravel. Let set 24 hours.
3. Using a flat lid as a template, cut out 2" thick circle of floral foam for dried or silk flowers.
4. Push a wooden skewer in the foam to create holes for tiny lights. Thread in lights through the holes and knot all cords together on top of floral foam. Push foam into neck of jar with 1/2" above neck of jar.
5. Glue battery pack to back of jar. Tie green raffia at neck of jar to hold wires in place.

Continued on page 54

continued from page 52

EMBELLISHMENTS

1. Arrange silk ferns, ivy, and greenery in floral foam.

Add dragonfly pick.
2. Use Spanish moss to cover visible floral foam, attaching moss with U-pins. ❏

Example of Stamped Paper for Peek-a-Boo Forest

Old-fashioned Label Jar

pictured on next page

JAR TYPE

Quart-size old-fashioned canning jar with glass lid and wire bail

JAR DECORATION

1. Adhere a selection of old labels (cut from decoupage paper) to jar with decoupage medium. Let dry.
2. Apply crackle finish, following manufacturer's instructions.
3. Antique with oil-base brown paint. Let dry.
4. Apply a two-part resin coating to jar to seal. ❏

You can add design and pattern to jars almost instantly with rub-on transfers, stickers, and rubber stamps. For adding sheen and metallic gleam, try metal leafing. This section includes information about each decorating material.

DECORATING JARS
with Rub-on Transfers, Stickers, Rubber Stamps & Metal Leafing

■ Rub-on Transfers

Transfers are an almost effortless way to decorate a jar. Motifs are available in many different themes and holiday patterns. For examples, see the Cookie Magic Jar and the Beachfront Property Jar.

Here's How:
1. Cut out the motif.
2. Place it, printed side down, on the clean jar surface.
3. Rub the transfer (this is called "burnishing") with a wooden craft stick (provided in transfer package) until the image is transferred to the surface.
4. Remove the backing paper carefully to reveal the design. *Tip:* I make sure the design is completely adhered by taking a piece of the tissue-like protective paper, covering the motif, and further burnishing with the craft stick.

■ Stickers & Labels

Stickers and pre-printed labels in many sizes, shapes, colors, and styles are available to decorate jars and gift tags. You can also design and make your own stickers and labels with photocopies of photographs and printed motifs and adhere them with double-sided adhesive paper or laminating sheets. (This is especially handy if making and decorating lots of jars for gifts or to sell.) The Knitting Jar was decorated with self-stick labels.

TIPS

for Using Stickers & Labels

• Make sure your jar surface is clean and grease-free.

• Some labels or stickers need to wrap around the jar and stick to themselves – they will pull away from the jar. Take that into account when designing your jar.

■ Rubber Stamps

The range of motifs available in rubber stamps is huge; whatever motif or theme you are looking for, there's probably a stamp available! The stamps are available in tiny sizes that can be repeated to create a design, or in large sizes for instant coverage. I use small stamps to make decorative seals from polymer clay.

■ Metal Leafing

Metal leafing, available at crafts stores and stores that sell art supplies, can be used to add accents and sheen to jars, labels, lids, and gift tags. You can use liquid leaf adhesive, spray adhesive, or double-sided tape to adhere leafing.

SUPPLIES

Gold, copper, or variegated gold leaf (available in fine art supply stores)
Leaf adhesive *or* spray adhesive *or* double-sided tape
Soft brush
Freezer paper

HERE'S HOW:

1. Protect your surface with freezer paper.
2. Apply adhesive to surface.
   With leaf adhesive: Brush a thin coat of adhesive on the surface you wish to leaf. Follow the manufacturer's instructions for how long the adhesive should dry.
   With spray adhesive: Lightly spray the adhesive on the surface you wish to leaf.
   With double-sided tape: Position the tape. Remove the protective paper.
3. Carefully place the leaf on the tacky surface. See photo 2.
4. Using a soft brush, gently brush leaf to smooth it onto adhesive. See photo 3.
5. Run a clean, dry brush over the leaf edges to remove excess flakes of leaf. ❏

Photo 1

Photo 2

This is a great bridal shower gift or a way to introduce a teenager to the joys of knitting and crocheting. It's also a great place to store a ball of twine!

Knitting Jar

Contents: Skein of natural cotton yarn, bamboo crochet hook, and instructions for making a crocheted or knitted dishcloth.

JAR TYPE
Plastic storage jar with white metal lid

JAR DECORATION
Affix a textile-theme self-adhesive sticker. (This one is a vintage label reproduction.)

LID DECORATION
1. Cut an antique label reproduction sticker to fit the top of the lid.

2. Punch a hole in the center with large nail. Insert a silver eyelet to finish hole.

3. Glue natural cotton twill tape around rim.

EMBELLISHMENTS
1. Wrap three types of yarn around 1" diameter plastic foam balls. Roll the ball in your hand to compress (make smaller).

2. Glue to side of jar.

3. Accent with small "knitting needles" made from wooden toothpicks with small wooden beads glued on one end of each. ❏

Polymer clay is easy to work with, comes in a wide range of colors, and can be baked in your home oven. Baked polymer clay objects can be varnished, painted, sanded, and drilled.

DECORATING WITH POLYMER CLAY

Use polymer clay to decorate lids with faux carved ivory, to make labels, and to make items to decorate the inside of a jar. (See the following list for project examples). New molds make it even easier to create decorations for your jars.

Project Examples

- Molded three-dimensional accents - Magic Beans Jar, Is It Coffee Yet? Jar
- Rolled clay leaf accents - Faux Etched Glass Tea Jar
- Faux carved ivory - Tuscan Market Jar, Mediterranean Herbs Jar, Italian Countryside Jars
- Rolled clay label - Magic Beans Jar
- An item to go in a jar - Beachfront Property Lamp Jar

Supplies

Polymer clay
Wooden roller (used exclusively for polymer clay, never for food)
Wooden craft and molding sticks
Polymer clay knife
Decorative molds (made to use with polymer clay)
Ceramic tile (for a work surface)
Optional: Pasta machine (used exclusively for polymer clay, never for food) A pasta machine makes conditioning and rolling out the clay easier and faster. It is a wise investment if you enjoy creating with this medium.

How to Decorate

1. Condition the clay, working it with your hands until it warms up and becomes more pliable. (You must do this before trying to roll or mold it.)
2. Roll out and form the clay. Use a knife for cutting a shape or mold the clay with your fingers or in a mold. *Tip:* A light dusting of corn-starch in decorative molds prevents the clay from sticking.
3. Bake in your oven according to the manufacturer's instructions. Be sure you have sufficient ventilation during baking.
4. When the clay object has cooled, decorate according to project instructions.

Pictured above: Polymer clay, molds and stamps for working with clay, molded and stamped clay pieces.

This jar is filled with flavored jelly beans. Kids love to make up names for the weird and wonderful flavors that go with the different colored beans.

Magic Beans Jar

Contents: Different colors of jelly beans, layered in the jar

JAR TYPE
Glass decorative candy jar with wooden lid

LID DECORATION
1. Remove rubber ring from lid. Cover lid with a thin layer of polymer clay.
2. Using a polymer clay mold, mold the face and hand. Add hair and details. Position on lid.
3. Using alphabet rubber stamps, press the words "MAGIC BEANS" into the clay. Bake according to manufacturer's directions. Let cool.
4. Paint with acrylic paints. Let dry.
5. Varnish. Let dry. Re-attach the rubber ring.

The Faux Carved Ivory Technique

YOU'LL NEED:
Basic Supplies listed above, *plus*
White craft glue
Acrylic craft paints - ivory, brown
Acrylic varnish
Optional: Crackle medium
Glue brush
Paint brushes
Cloth rags

Several projects in this book use faux carved ivory made from polymer clay to decorate jar lids. Using the same lid decoration technique can make a "set" from a group of different-sized jars. The technique can be used to decorate wooden or glass lids.

HERE'S HOW:
1. Condition the clay. Roll out thin sheets large enough to cover the tops of the wooden or glass lids.
2. Brush a little glue on the tops of the lids. Place the rolled clay over the lids. Trim to fit.
3. Make the decorative pieces by pushing the clay into the molds to create the shapes. Unmold shapes and arrange on the lids.
4. Bake the lid in the oven to harden. Let cool.
5. Paint the lids with two coats ivory acrylic paint.
6. *Option:* Use crackle medium for a decorative crackle effect at this time.
7. Antique the lids by brushing on a coat of brown acrylic paint thinned with water. Rub off the excess paint with a cloth.
8. Give the lids a coat of acrylic varnish for an attractive, protective finish.

Speckled Green...Newt
Speckled White...Freckle
Red......Peppermint
Dark Green...Dragon Breath
Orange...Marmalade

EMBELLISHMENTS

1. Wrap a yard of gold star garland around the neck of the jar.

2. To make the label, roll polymer clay very thin and wrap and curl to form what looks like an old parchment scroll. Make two small holes at the top of the scroll. Bake according to the manufacturer's directions. Let cool. Write the list of colors and flavors with a permanent black pen. Thread gold cord through the holes and hang on the front of the jar. ❑

Molded polymer clay and real coffee beans decorate the top of this jar. It could also be filled with coffee beans.

Is It Coffee Yet?

JAR TYPE

Old fashioned glass canning jar with glass lid and wire bail.

JAR DECORATION

Tie a coffee brown ribbon around neck of jar.

LID DECORATION

1. Mold face, hands, and banner from polymer clay. (A face mold was used for the face. A mustache was added and detailed with a wooden skewer. The banner was molded from a thin sheet of clay.) Stamp banner with "Is it coffee yet?" using alphabet rubber stamps.
2. Press fresh leaves into pieces of polymer clay to make leaf shapes. Cut out leaves.
3. Arrange face, hands, banner, and leaves on jar lid. Press some coffee beans among the leaves.
4. Bake the jar with the clay pieces on the lid in an oven according to manufacturer's instructions. Let cool.
5. Paint clay pieces with acrylic craft paints. Let dry.
6. Apply a resin coating, following the instructions in the section titled "Making Resin-coated Jars & Lids."

Contents: Cappuccino Coffee Mix

EMBELLISHMENTS

Print "Cup of Cappuccino" instructions on a card. (See the "Drink Mixes" section for text.) Laminate and punch with a small hole. Attach to neck of jar with brown elastic cording. ❏

RECIPE

Cappuccino Mix

This makes 2-1/4 cups.

1/2 cup sugar
1/4 cup cocoa
1/2 cup powdered coffee whitener
1/2 cup instant coffee
1/2 cup skim milk powder
1 teaspoon cinnamon
1/4 teaspoon nutmeg

Layer ingredients in a jar. ❏

Cup of Cappuccino

Makes 1 cup.

Cappuccino Mix
Ground nutmeg
Cinnamon sticks

Stir contents of jar before measuring. Measure 2 tablespoons Cappuccino Mix and place in blender. Add 1 cup boiling water. Process until foamy. Sprinkle with nutmeg. Use cinnamon sticks to stir. ❏

Spiced Mocha Coffee

Makes 1 serving.

1 tablespoon Spiced Mocha Coffee Mix
6 ounces boiling water
Shaved chocolate
Cinnamon stick

Place the coffee mix in the bottom of a coffee mug. Pour in boiling water. Stir to mix. Garnish with shaved chocolate and a cinnamon stick. ❏

RECIPE

Spiced Mocha Coffee Mix

Makes 1-1/3 cups.

1/3 cup instant coffee
1/2 cup cocoa
1/2 cup nonfat dry milk

1 teaspoon ground cinnamon
2 teaspoons dried orange peel

Layer the ingredients in a half-pint jar. Present with a bar of chocolate and cinnamon sticks. ❏

Well-chosen embellishments make jars look professional and finished. Fabric and crafts stores carry a huge variety of items that can be used to embellish your jars.

EMBELLISHMENTS for Jars

The following are some of my favorites; perhaps you already have some of your own.

■ Ribbon

Ribbon is (by far) the easiest trimming to work with and coordinate with a project. A huge variety of widths, colors, styles, and textures await your creative touch.

■ Charms

Charms are available in a wide range of metallic finishes and motifs. Use silicone-based glue designed for metal to adhere the charms to jars and lids.

You can also find beautiful embossed pewter labels and charms with adhesive backing. These are especially handy for adhering to a curved glass surface, as they will bend.

■ Buttons

Plastic buttons come in a wide range of motifs and colors. Buttons with holes or shank buttons can be used; use wire cutters to remove the shank so the back of the button is flat. Use silicon-based glue to adhere buttons.

■ Decorative Seals

You can buy pre-made seals or make them from sealing wax, but I like making my own seals with polymer clay and small rubber stamps. I usually make many seals at one sitting, so I have a selection handy when I'm ready to decorate a jar or wrap a gift.

Here's how:
1. Condition a small (3/4") piece of clay into a ball and flatten slightly.
2. Push the rubber stamp into the clay to make the decorative impression.
3. Bake the clay according to the manufacturer's instructions.
4. After your seal has cooled, you can paint it and/or antique it with acrylic craft paint.

■ Metallic Bullion

Bullion is a very fine wire that has been wrapped into a thin coil. It comes in gold, silver, copper, red, and green hues. Bullion was used in Victorian times to accent Christmas

decorations and as tree tinsel. To use, cut a small (3") piece and stretch it to produce a kinky thread of metallic wire. You can wrap the wire around jars or decorations or twist it into a bow and glue to a project. Look for it at florist's supply stores and specialty Christmas retailers.

■ Tassels

Fabric stores, home decor outlets, and craft stores stock tassels in a wide variety of sizes and colors. You can make plain tassels more elaborate by adding fused pearls, ribbon roses, or charms.

It's easy and economical to make your own tassels by winding and gluing a lampshade fringe around the knotted end of a length of cord. You can also make tassels from beads, pieces of ribbon, and a variety of fringe colors to make tassels.

French Lavender Bath Salts Jar

Contents: Lavender Bath Salts. For the Lavender Bath Salts Recipe, see below.

JAR TYPE

Pint-size canning jar with a two-piece lid (flat seal and band)

JAR DECORATION

1. Paint a simple border of flowering lavender along the top and bottom of the jar with purple and green paint pens.
2. Write "La Lavande" (French for "The Lavender") around the jar between the borders with a green paint pen.

LID DECORATION

1. Cut decorative paper to fit on top of the flat lid.
2. Glue satin ribbon around edge of band. Wrap 30" of cording over ribbon and glue in place.

EMBELLISHMENTS

1. To make the gift tag, cut a 2-1/2" x 4" piece of decorative paper. Fold to make a card. Rubber stamp a lavender basket motif on a 1-1/2" x 1" cream panel. Outline with a marker to make a "frame." Glue to folded card. Punch a hole in the corner of the tag. Add a loop of thin gold cord and attach to the jar.
2. Paint a small wooden scoop with cream acrylic craft paint. Paint the handle and edge with soft, muted green. Decorate with paint pens, using a stencil to make gold fleur de lis motifs. Accent with purple dots made with a paint pen. Tie gold elastic cord around the handle of the scoop and loop around neck of jar. ❑

Making Bath Salts

Bath salts are easy to make – the ingredients can be found in grocery stores, drugstores, health food stores, and crafts shops. You simply mix a fixative (Epsom salt, rock salt, sea salt, baking soda) with scent (essential oils or fragrance oils) and color (food coloring – but adding color is optional).

Everything you need in the way of equipment you probably already have in your kitchen: glass or metal bowls for mixing, metal spoons for mixing and measuring, glass measuring cups, paper towels for wiping up, and a small bottle to help you pack the salts in the jar.

RECIPE

Lavender Bath Salts

These layered bath salts are colored and scented in three batches.

1-1/2 cups Epsom salt	Colorants - blue, red food coloring
1-1/2 cups rock salt	Fragrance oils - lavender, rose

First layer: Mix 1/2 cup Epsom salt and 1/2 cup rock salt. Color with 4 drops blue and 3 drops red colorants (dark lavender). Scent with 15 drops lavender fragrance oil.

Second layer: Mix 1/2 cup Epsom salt and 1/2 cup rock salt. Color with 3 drops red colorant (light pink). Scent with 10 drops rose fragrance oil.

Third layer: 1/2 cup Epsom salts and 1/2 cup rock salt. (No colorant is added.) Scent with 15 drops lavender fragrance oil.

To use bath salts: Draw a warm bath and, as you fill the tub, add the fragrant salts to the running water. Hop in and relax, inhaling deeply to experience the refreshing and soothing aromas. ❑

Pictured above, left to right: Spa in a Jar, French Lavender Bath Salts Jar. Instructions for "Spa in a Jar" follow on next page.

This large jar is packed with everything you need for a relaxing "spa day" – even a rubber ducky for the bath!

Spa in a Jar

Contents: Bath and grooming aids, such as handmade milled soaps, a sea sponge, a natural nail brush, wooden comb, sisal washcloth, hand-formed lavender soap balls, bath oil beads (in yellow duck or other shapes), a rubber ducky, loofah sponge, soft nylon body scrubber, and bags of lavender buds (muslin bags stamped with a lavender stamp)

JAR TYPE

Gallon-size recycled jar (no lid)

LID DECORATION

1. Weave a 1/2" wide ecru satin ribbon 1" from the edge of a 6" round crocheted doily.
2. Pull up the ribbon so the doily fits over the neck of the jar. Tie in a bow.

EMBELLISHMENTS

1. Add a cord with tassels. To make the tassels, cut one 20" piece of ivory cord and two pieces, each 4" long, of 3-1/2" ivory lampshade fringe. Tie a knot at each end of the cord. Place a line of glue along the top edge of the fringe and tightly wrap fringe around the ends of the cord. Let dry.
2. Further embellish each tassel with fused pearl trim and a gold ribbon rose.
3. To make tags, cut a 3" x 7" piece of cream paper. Decorate with rubber-stamped decorative motifs. Punch a hole the corner of the tag. Attach to the jar with a loop of thin gold cord. ❏

Sewing Jar

A sewing apron adorned with sewing-themed charms and buttons decorates this jar filled with sewing tools and notions. The lid has an attached pin cushion; an "apron" with pockets can hold notions. It's pretty enough to display and keep handy for mending projects.

Contents: Sewing notions, such as a needle case made from two pieces of felt in coordinating colors, skeins of pearl embroidery cotton, lace, a tracing wheel, a thimble, a measuring tape, scissors

JAR TYPE

Quart-size canning jar with two-piece lid

JAR DECORATION

1. To make the jar apron, cut a 6-1/2" x 11-1/2" piece of fabric. Press a 1/4" hem on all raw edges.
   Stitch or glue hems.
2. Fold fabric piece in half. Place a 12" piece elastic cord inside at the fold. Sew or glue crocheted lace around hemmed edges.
3. Cut three pockets, each 2-1/2" square. Press under 1/4" hems all around. Sew to apron.
4. Using fabric glue, add sewing-themed plastic buttons (shanks removed) or charms (thread spools, scissors, tape measure) to pockets. Make a small ribbon bow and attach plastic dress form.
5. Slip apron over jar.

LID DECORATION

1. Cut a fabric circle 7" in diameter. Sew a running stitch with strong thread 1/2" from edge. Pull to gather and stuff with polyester pillow stuffing. Place over flat lid and pull tightly around edges of lid. Place metal band on lid and glue to lid. Place lid assembly on jar and screw tightly to hold while drying.

2. Glue crocheted lace (a scrap or a piece cut from old hankie) around outside of band. Glue plastic charms or buttons with shanks removed (thimble, needle, various buttons in coordinating colors) to accent.

Pictured above: Knitting Jar, Sewing Jar. See page 58 for Knitting Jar instructions.

EMBELLISHMENTS

To make a gift tag, fold a 2-1/2" x 5" piece of cream card stock in half. Decorate with a 2" square white panel. Glue a button (shank removed) in the center and add a plastic needle charm. Write "From my hands to your heart" with felt pen. ❑

MAKING RESIN-COATED JARS & LIDS

A two-part pour-on resin coating gives decoupaged paper, polymer clay, and various embellishments (such as popcorn, coffee beans, or charms) a hard, waterproof finish with a depth and luster equal to 50 coats of varnish. I use it for many projects to provide a professional finish and a practical, easy-to-clean surface. The procedure is easy, and the results are spectacular.

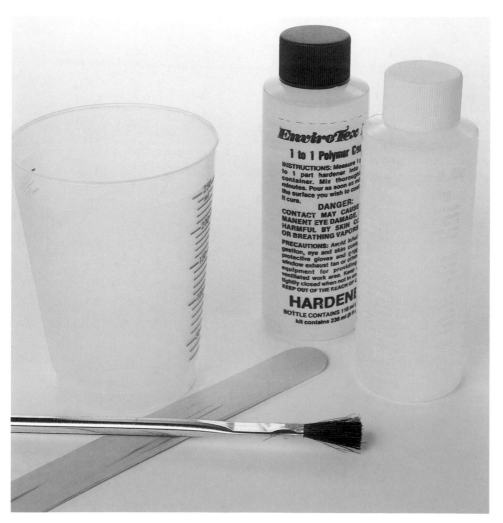

Supplies

Two-part pour-on resin coating

plus a mixing cup, a wooden stir stick, and an inexpensive glue brush. (All these items will be discarded after use.)

Freezer paper or wax paper, to protect your work surface

Plastic or wax **paper cups**, to prop up your project and keep it off the work surface

Thin-bodied white glue (the kind that dries clear) or clear cellophane tape to attach decorations to surface.

Here's How:

1. Protect the underside of the jar with rubber cement or cellophane tape.

2. Seal all decorative treatments on the jar (paper and all porous materials, such as food items) that you plan to cover with the resin coating with a coat of thin-bodied white glue. Simply brush on the glue. While it is drying, place the jar, right side up, on a waxed paper cup to lift it off your work surface.

3. When the glue is dry, you are ready to mix the resin coating. The coating comes in two parts, the resin and the hardener. Mix only as much as you can use on your project as leftover material cannot be saved for other projects. Measure out the two parts in the same container. You want to mix exactly 1 part resin with 1 part hardener. See photo 1.

4. Mix the resin and hardener with a wooden stick until thoroughly blended – this takes a full two minutes of vigorous mixing. The importance of thorough mixing cannot be over-emphasized, as poor mixing can cause the coating to not harden properly. When bubbles appear in the mixture, they can be removed after the resin is poured.

5. As soon as the resin coating is mixed, pour it over the outside of your jar. See photo 2. Allow excess to drip off onto protected surface.

6. Spread, using the brush, where necessary. You will have about 10 minutes to work on your project before the coating starts to set up.

7. After about 5 minutes, the air bubbles created during mixing will rise to the surface. They can be easily and effectively broken by gently exhaling on them until they disappear. (The carbon dioxide in your breath breaks the bubbles.) **Avoid inhaling the fumes** while you de-gas the bubbles.

8. Allow your project to cure for a full 72 hours to a hard and permanent finish. Remove the tape or rubber cement from the bottom of the jar. Sand off any drips with fine grade sandpaper. Discard the mixing cup, the stir stick, and the brush. ❑

CAUTIONS & CONSIDERATIONS

- Your work surface should be level and the area warm and free of dust.
- Your project surface should be dry and free of any dust or grease.
- The coating will drip off the sides of the project. Protect the underside by brushing on some rubber cement or covering the bottom edges with clear cellophane tape.
- If drips occur on an unprotected surface, they can be sanded off when the finish has cured.

Photo 1

Photo 2

Treat jars can be decorated with resin-coated contents on the lids for a whimsical touch. Change the tops to suit your taste.

Popcorn Jar

Contents: Candied Popcorn (See the "Treats" recipe section.)

JAR TYPE

Glass decorative jar with wooden top

JAR DECORATION

1. Glue a 12" ochre-colored grosgrain ribbon around the neck.
2. Tie 1 yard of thin white satin ribbon around the neck. Make a multi-loop bow in front.

LID DECORATION

1. Pop some popcorn. Let cool.
2. Using white glue, glue popcorn and some unpopped kernels to wooden lid. Brush the popcorn and kernels with white glue to seal. Let dry.
3. Pour a two-part resin coating over the lid to finish.

EMBELLISHMENTS

To make the gift tag, write "Popcorn" and outline some popped corn pieces on white. Color letters with a yellow marker. Cut out, then mount on yellow paper. Punch a hole and attach to jar with thin gold cording. ❑

Pictured right: Popcorn Jar, Nuts 'n Bolts Jar

RECIPE

Candied Popcorn
Makes 6 cups of popped corn

2 cups sugar
2 cups light brown sugar, firmly packed
2 cups light cream
1 teaspoon soft butter
3/4 teaspoon vanilla
1/2 cup whole almonds or pecans
6 cups popped popcorn, with unpopped kernels removed

Combine sugars and cream. Stir until sugar is dissolved. Boil uncovered without stirring until syrup reaches soft-ball stage (235-240 degrees F.) Cool for 10 minutes.

Beat with a wooden spoon until thickened. Add vanilla and nuts and popcorn and mix well. Pour on sheets of parchment paper to cool. Break apart larger pieces and package in airtight jars. ❑

This jar is a great hit as a gift at holidays or any other time of the year, and it also contains a favorite "manly" treat.

Nuts 'n Bolts Jar

pictured on page 75

Contents: Nuts 'n Bolts (See the "Treats" recipe section.)

JAR TYPE

Quart-size canning jar with two-part lid

LID DECORATION

1. Paint both parts of the lid (seal and band), using an "instant rust" paint kit. Let dry.
2. Glue a selection of rusty nuts, bolts, and screws (a great way to use the contents of your "miscellaneous" jar) to the seal with silicone glue. Let dry.
3. Pour a two-part resin coating over the lid to finish. Let dry.
4. Tie natural raffia around the band.

EMBELLISHMENTS

To make gift tag, cut a 2-1/2" x 5" piece of natural parchment paper. Fold to make a square card. Cut a 1-1/2" square panel from rust colored paper with decorative edge scissors. Make a seal with polymer clay or sealing wax and glue to the card. Write "Nuts 'n Bolts" around the panel with a black pen. ❑

RECIPE

Nuts 'n Bolts

This is my husband's favorite — we call this recipe "Scott's Legendary Nuts 'n Bolts." It has become a tradition for him to make this for everyone on our list.

2 lbs. salted mixed nuts
3 cups round oat cereal (Cheerios)
2 cups pretzel sticks
3 cups mini shredded wheat cereal
3 cups crispy squares cereal (Life or Rice Chex)
1 tablespoon Worcestershire sauce
1/2 tablespoon garlic powder
1 tablespoon seasoning salt
1 cup peanut oil

Mix the Worcestershire sauce, garlic powder, seasoning salt, and peanut oil in a bowl. Mix cereals and pretzel sticks in another bowl. Pour the spiced oil over the cereal mixture and stir to coat. Bake in the oven at 250 degrees F. for 2 hours, stirring every 15 minutes. ❑

Try these recipes for more fun treat jars.

Roasted Nuts

For those who like a savory and salty treat rather than a sweet indulgence.

1 tablespoon butter
2 tablespoons ketchup
2 tablespoons Worcestershire sauce
1/4 teaspoon cayenne pepper
1/4 teaspoon garlic salt
2 cups whole pecans or almonds

Melt butter. Add ketchup, Worcestershire sauce, cayenne pepper, and garlic salt. Mix well. Add nuts and stir until nuts are well-coated. Spread on greased baking sheet. Bake in the oven at 350 degrees F. for 20 minutes. ❑

Candied Pretzels Recipe

*This is sweet **and** salty.*

1 package mini twist pretzels
2 cups nuts
1 cup unsalted butter
2 cups brown sugar
1/2 cup light corn syrup
Pinch salt

Preheat oven to 250 degrees F. Combine pretzels and nuts; set aside. Combine butter, sugar, syrup, and salt. Bring to boil and cook until very thick. Pour sugar mixture over pretzels and nuts. Place on a greased cookie sheet. Bake in oven for 20 minutes, stirring after 10 minutes. Remove from oven and spread on wax paper to cool. ❑

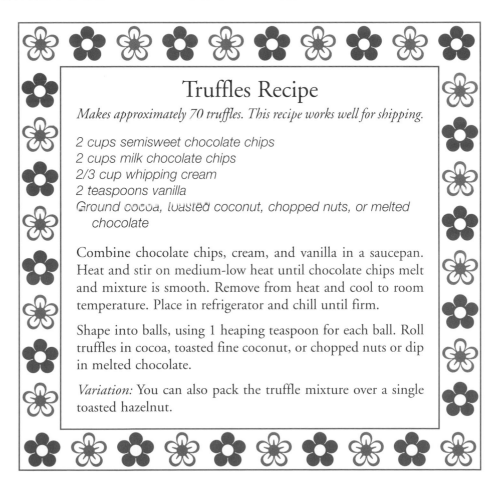

Truffles Recipe

Makes approximately 70 truffles. This recipe works well for shipping.

2 cups semisweet chocolate chips
2 cups milk chocolate chips
2/3 cup whipping cream
2 teaspoons vanilla
Ground cocoa, toasted coconut, chopped nuts, or melted
    chocolate

Combine chocolate chips, cream, and vanilla in a saucepan. Heat and stir on medium-low heat until chocolate chips melt and mixture is smooth. Remove from heat and cool to room temperature. Place in refrigerator and chill until firm.

Shape into balls, using 1 heaping teaspoon for each ball. Roll truffles in cocoa, toasted fine coconut, or chopped nuts or dip in melted chocolate.

Variation: You can also pack the truffle mixture over a single toasted hazelnut.

Handcrafted labels and tags add interest to jars, convey useful information, and are a lovely way to further personalize a gift. In this chapter you will find examples of cards and tags to create and you will learn how to make metal tags for a unique addition to special jars.

MAKING LABELS, RECIPE CARDS & TAGS

When you take the time to create a decorated jar of layered cookie or soup mix, make sure you give the same attention to labeling the jars' contents and including instructions for preparing the mixes so the recipient will know what's in your gift and how to use it.

Sugar 'n Spice Nuts Recipe

This very easy recipe combines spices with sugar for a not-too-sweet nut.

1/2 cup brown sugar
1/2 cup sugar
1 teaspoon cinnamon
1/2 teaspoon ginger
1/2 teaspoon nutmeg
1 egg white
1 tablespoon water
l teaspoon vanilla
4 cups pecans or mixed nuts

Combine sugars and spices. Beat egg white and water until frothy. Add sugar and spice mixture. Add nuts. Spread on greased baking sheet and bake in the oven at 325 degrees F. for 20 minutes, stirring occasionally. The nuts should look dry and slightly browned. ❏

You can hand-write your labels and recipes on cards or type them and print them out on a computer on 8-1/2" x 11" sheets of card stock. Or print them on plain paper and mount them on a slightly larger piece of decorative paper to create an attractive "frame." You can further decorate your labels and cards with paint, stenciling, rubber stamps, rub-on transfers, and stickers. If you're making lots of jars for gifts, you may wish to create a page of decorated labels or cards and have them duplicated at a copy shop. (Doing them a page at a time can save money.)

Laminating recipe cards with laminating film or a laminating machine is a practical touch. To attach to the jar, punch a hole in the card or label and add a thin elastic cord.

Trail Bean Soup

1 jar **Bean Soup Mix**
2 quarts water
1 ham hock
1 ¼ teaspoon salt
1 teaspoon pepper
1 can diced tomatoes
1 large onion, chopped
1 minced garlic glove

Soak beans in 2 cups water overnight. Bring water and ham hock to boil. Simmer 20 minutes. Remove ham hock. Drain beans; stir in rest of ingredients. Bring to boil, reduce heat, and simmer 1 hour.

Chocolate Gingerbread Folks
Makes about 2 dozen cookies

1 package **Gingerbread Cookie Mix**
1/2 cup molasses
1/2 cup butter
1/4 cup hot water

Preheat the oven to 375° F. Place sieve onto of bowl a shake out chocolate pieces. Combine molasses, butter and chocolate in double boiler and heat until chocolate is melted. Stir smooth. Stir in hot water and then mix in dry ingredients. Mix well; chill until firm (2 hours). Cut the dough into quarters and work with 1/4 at a time. Roll the dough to a 1/4" thickness on a floured board. Cut into gingerbread men shapes and place on an ungreased cookie sheet. Bake for 8 minutes. Repeat...

Tuscan Market Soup

1 Jar **Tuscan market Soup Mix**
2 stalks Celery
2 sliced Carrots
1 cup shredded cabbage
1 can crushed tomatoes

Add contents of jar to 3 quarts water and the vegetables. Over med. heat, cover and simmer 1 hour until vegetables tender.

Cup of Cappuccino

Makes 1 cup.

Cappuccino Mix
Ground nutmeg
Cinnamon sticks

Stir contents of jar before measuring. Measure 2 tablespoons Cappuccino Mix and place in blender. Add 1 cup boiling water. Process until foamy. Sprinkle with nutmeg. Use cinnamon sticks to stir.

Mediterranean Herb Vinaigrette

1 tablespoon Mediterranean Herb Blend
1/4 cup olive oil
Juice of one lemon

Mix all ingredients. Refrigerate for a few hours to allow the flavors to blend. Stir to mix well before pouring on salad greens or grilled vegetables.

BEST-EVER COOKIES

Makes 4 dozen.

1 jar Best-Ever Cookie Mix
1 cup butter
2 teaspoons vanilla extract
2 eggs

Preheat the oven to 375 degrees F. Using an electric mixer, cream the butter, eggs, and vanilla. Add the cookie mix and stir until well blended. Drop the cookies by rounded tablespoonfuls on an ungreased cookie sheet. Bake for 8 to 10 minutes, until golden brown. Transfer to a wire rack to cool. ❏

RANCH DIP

Makes 2 cups.

2 tablespoons Ranch Dressing Mix
1 cup mayonnaise
1 cup sour cream

Combine all ingredients in a bowl. Refrigerate for 2 hours. Serve as a dip for raw vegetables or as a topping for baked potatoes. ❏

RANCH DRESSING

Makes 1 cup.

1 tablespoon Ranch Dressing Mix
1/2 cup mayonnaise
1/2 cup buttermilk

Whisk all ingredients together in a bowl. Refrigerate for 1 hour before serving. ❏

TAGS

Most of the gift tags for the projects in this book are made of cardweight paper and are decorated with layered paper panels. I use decorative-edge scissors to cut panels with interesting edges and decorate them with a variety of embellishments, including paint, stenciling, rub-on transfers, decorative seals, rubber stamps, metal charms, and plastic buttons.

I use gel pens or felt-tip pens to add lettering and greetings to tags. Hole punches in different shapes (stars, hearts, squares, etc.) can add interest to cards. Use thin elastic cording, thin ribbon, or string to attach tags to jars.

Metal tags can be used as decorations or as labels. Metal tags are cut from metal sheets and embossed. The sheets are available in aluminum (silver-colored), copper, or brass (gold-colored).

Pictured above: Metal sheets, embossing tool

Metal Tags

SUPPLIES

36 gauge metal sheets (aluminum, copper, or brass)

Embossing tool (or a ballpoint pen)

Soft pad (a piece of foam sheeting, a carpet sample, or the foam back of a computer mousepad, for example)

Metal paints

20 gauge wire

Tin snips or old scissors

Hole punch or awl

HERE'S HOW:

1. Cut out the metal shape with tin snips or old scissors.
2. Place the metal on a soft pad. "Write" the design, using an embossing tool or a ballpoint pen.
3. Use metal paints to add details or enhance the color.
4. Use a hole punch or awl to make a hole in the tag.
5. Use 20-gauge wire to attach the metal tag to the jar. ❑

Culinary Gifts

Culinary gifts are a way to share a favorite recipe, and they give the recipient two gifts – the gift of something delicious to eat, and the gift of time.

My recipes come from many sources – my family, my friends, and my adaptations of personal favorites – all tested in my kitchen and approved by the critical taste-testings of family members. I tried to make the recipes both traditional and unique, so the idea is familiar and appealing, but the gift is one that cannot be bought in a store.

Making your own mixes saves money and gives the opportunity to reduce preservatives, additives, salt, and sugar in the finished product. Each mix recipe comes with food recipe (or two) to package with the mix. Be sure to add a recipe card, laminated for an extra practical touch, and a list of all the ingredients. Make the jar embellishments for culinary gifts practical ones, such as a gingerbread man cookie cutter attached to a jar of Gingerbread Cookie Mix or a tea ball on a jar of tea.

Basic Procedures
for Making Culinary Gifts

Sterilizing Jars

The jars you use to package food gifts should be sterilized before use. Here's how:

1. Check all jars for chips and cracks. If chipped or cracked, don't use for food. Check lids for dents or rust. If dented or rusty, don't use for food.

2. Wash all parts with hot, soapy water. Rinse.
3. To sterilize jars, place on a rack in large pot and cover with water. Let water come to a boil and boil for 15 minutes. Remove and dry completely before filling. *Option:* You can also sterilize jars and lids in the dishwasher.

Continued on page 86

Pictured left to right: Gingerbread Cookie Jar, Cookie Magic Jar, and Cowboy Brownies Jar

COOKIES

Preheat the oven to 375°F. With an electric
mixer, cream the butter, eggs and vanilla. Add
the cookie mix and stir until well blended.
Drop the cookies by rounded tablespoonfuls
onto an ungreased cookie sheet. Bake for 8 to
10 minutes until golden brown and transfer to
a baking rack to cool.

continued from page 84

FILLING JARS

Culinary mixes often look better when the ingredients for the mix are layered in the jar. The recipient can mix the ingredients before using them.

Basic Equipment for Filling Jars

• Wooden spoons for mixing

• Large spoon for filling jars

• Small bottle for tamping down the ingredients as you layer or place them in the jar

• Paper towels for wiping powdery ingredients off jars

• A canning funnel (available at stores where canning supplies are sold) or a piece of card stock to make a simple funnel for filling the jars

General Tips for Packaging Homemade Mixes

• Layer ingredients in the jar in the order given in the recipe.

• Wipe down the sides of the jar with a clean paper towel after adding powdery ingredients, such as powdered (icing) sugar, cocoa, or flour before adding the next ingredient for a better appearance.

• Pack down all ingredients firmly. If you don't, you won't have enough space to fit in all the ingredients. (You will be surprised at how flour packs down!) Generally, a quart jar holds 6 cups of packed down ingredients; a pint jar holds 3 cups packed down ingredients. This is, however, a very general observation, as each recipe is made up of different ingredients that all pack down differently.

• If your ingredients do not come to the top of the jar, fill with crumpled plastic wrap or wax paper to prevent the ingredients from shifting and mixing.

Storing Culinary Mixes

Cool, dry storage is best. **Never** store finished jars near a heat source, hot pipes, stove, or furnace or in direct sunlight. If you cannot guarantee cool and dry storage, it's better to store your mixes in the refrigerator.

One excellent quality of your homemade mixes is that they are preservative-free. For maximum freshness, label them with a "best before" date. Many factors determine the "best before" date, such as the type of flour (all-purpose flour has a longer shelf life than whole-wheat flour), preserving method (freshly dried herbs from your garden verses dried herbs bought from the market), and the general quality and freshness of the ingredients you use. These factors have been taken in account when suggesting these recommended best-before dates:

• Dressing, dip, and seasoning blends - 6 months

• Beans, dried vegetable soup blends - 3 months

• Bread, muffin, and scone mixes - 2 weeks in the refrigerator

• Cookie and cake mixes - 2 months; with nuts - 1 month

• Coffee and tea mixes - 3 months

Even though many mixes would last much longer than the suggested times, the strength of the colors and flavors will fade. The goal is to provide foods that are both safe and of high quality. Remember *quality* is not the same as *safety*. A poor-quality food (such as stale cereal) may be safe to eat; an unsafe food may look and taste good but contain harmful bacteria.

Substitutions

• Low-fat mayonnaise can be substituted for regular mayonnaise.

• Yogurt can be substituted for sour cream.

• Decaffeinated instant coffee can be substituted for regular instant coffee.

Oven Temperatures

• All oven temperatures are in degrees Fahrenheit. Unless it says otherwise, **always preheat** the oven.

Cookie mixes are a great addition to gift baskets. Keep a few jars on hand and when you need a quick gift, you'll have one. Recipes for the mixes and the cookies are included on the following pages.

Gingerbread Cookie Jar *pictured on page 85*

Contents: Chocolate Gingerbread Cookie Mix

JAR TYPE

Quart-size canning jar

LID DECORATION

1. Using pinking shears, cut a 7" circle of red fabric and a 5" circle of red fabric.
2. Center a 3" circle of 1/2" thick polyester batting on the 7" red fabric circle. Center a 6" round white doily on the batting. Place the 5" red fabric circle on top. Sew a red button sewn at the middle to hold all the pieces together. Place on jar lid.
3. Thread a 14" piece of gold elastic cord with gold beads, plastic "light bulb" beads, and star buttons. Knot ends to secure.
4. Place over fabric lid cover to hold it in place, wrapping the cord around the band twice.

EMBELLISHMENTS

1. Add a laminated card printed with the Chocolate Gingerbread Folks recipe and a copper gingerbread cookie cutter.
2. Make a gift tag that's also an ornament for the tree. Cut out (from 1/8" wood) or buy a 4" gingerbread man. Paint with metallic bronze paint. Glue on three red heart-shaped plastic buttons. Paint features and border on gingerbread man with metallic champagne fabric paint. ❏

Is it the jar or the cookies that are magic? The mix in this jar will make cookies that disappear right before your eyes! Look for the recipe on the following pages.

Cookie Magic Jar *pictured on page 85*

Contents: Layered cookie mix (Best-Ever Cookie Mix or Oatmeal Toffee Cookie Mix — recipes follow)

JAR TYPE

Quart-size clear recycled glass jar with white plastic lid

JAR DECORATION

Apply a cookie-themed rub-on transfer on the jar. The best area to put it is where the layer of flour is — the transfer will be more visible — so plan to layer the flour in the middle of the jar.

LID DECORATION

1. Glue 10" yellow grosgrain ribbon around the edge of the lid.
2. Accent ribbon with glued-on star and heart buttons (shanks removed).
3. Accent the top of the jar with a cookie-themed rub-on transfer.

EMBELLISHMENTS

1. Make a laminated label with directions for making the cookies. Accent with cookie-themed rub-on transfers.
2. For the gift tag, cut a 2" x 4" piece of white card stock. Decorate with a cookie-themed rub-on transfer.
3. Punch label and tag with a star punch. Attach to the jar with gold elastic cord. ❏

This recipe makes very rich, chocolate brownies for an extra sweet treat. Tie a 6" wooden skewer to the jar for the recipient to check when the brownies are done.

Cowboy Brownies Jar

Contents: Cowboy Brownie Mix (After layering ingredients, use a chopstick to make streaks through layers of ingredients.)

JAR TYPE

Quart-size canning jar with two-part lid

LID DECORATION

1. Cut a 7" circle from red bandanna-print fabric.
2. Place over lid. Wrap gold rope around neck of jar and tie to secure fabric.
3. Glue plastic cowboy-themed button on top.

EMBELLISHMENTS

1. To make the gift tag, stencil a 2" square panel of tan paper with cowboy boots or a cowboy hat. Ink a barbed wire border with a black pen. Cut a 2-1/2" x 5" card and fold. Glue panel to front of card.
2. Add a laminated brownie recipe card with stenciled accents. ❏

Chocolate Brownies

Makes 24.

1 jar Cowboy Brownie Mix
1 cup butter
4 eggs

Preheat the oven to 325 degrees F. Grease and flour a 13" x 9" pan. With an electric mixer, cream the butter. Add the eggs one at a time, beating well after each addition. Add the brownie mix and continue to mix by hand until smooth. Spread the mixture into the pan and bake 40 to 50 minutes until a wooden skewer comes out clean. ❑

Cowboy Brownie Mix

Makes 5-1/2 cups of mix.

2 cups sugar
1 cup cocoa powder
1 cup all-purpose flour
1 cup chopped pecans
1/2 cup chocolate chips

Layer the ingredients in a quart-size jar. ❑

Chocolate Gingerbread Cookie Mix

Makes 3 cups.

2-1/2 cups all-purpose flour
2/3 cup sugar
1-1/2 cups semi-sweet
   chocolate pieces
1/4 teaspoon salt
1/2 teaspoon baking soda
1 teaspoon ground ginger
1/4 teaspoon ground nutmeg

Sift the ingredients together. Place in a jar. ❑

Chocolate Gingerbread Folks

Makes about 2 dozen cookies.

1 jar Chocolate Gingerbread Cookie Mix
1/2 cup molasses
1/2 cup butter
1/4 cup hot water

Preheat the oven to 375 degrees F. Place a sieve on a mixing bowl. Pour mix through sieve to remove chocolate pieces. Combine molasses, butter, and chocolate in a double boiler and heat until chocolate is melted. Stir until smooth. Stir in hot water. Add dry ingredients and mix well. Chill in refrigerator until firm (about 2 hours).

Cut the dough in four pieces of equal size. On a floured board, working with one piece of dough at a time, roll the dough to a 1/4" thickness. Using a cookie cutter, cut in gingerbread man shapes. Place cookies on an ungreased cookie sheet. Bake for 8 to 10 minutes. Cool on a rack. Repeat with the remaining dough. ❑

Oatmeal Toffee Cookie Mix

Makes 4 cups.

1 cup brown sugar
1/3 cup sugar
1-1/2 cups all-purpose flour
1 teaspoon cinnamon
1 teaspoon baking soda
2 chocolate-covered toffee
*   candy bars, coarsely*
*   chopped*
3 cups rolled oats

Sift together the flour, baking soda, and cinnamon. Layer the flour mixture and all the other ingredients in a glass jar. ❏

Best-Ever Cookies

Makes 4 dozen.

1 jar Best-Ever Cookie Mix
1 cup butter
2 teaspoons vanilla extract
2 eggs

Preheat the oven to 375 degrees F. Using an electric mixer, cream the butter, eggs, and vanilla. Add the cookie mix and stir until well blended. Drop the cookies by rounded tablespoonfuls on an ungreased cookie sheet. Bake for 8 to 10 minutes, until golden brown. Transfer to a wire rack to cool. ❏

Oatmeal Toffee Cookies

Makes 4 dozen cookies.

1 jar Oatmeal Toffee Cookie Mix
1-1/4 cups butter
1 egg
1 teaspoon vanilla

Preheat the oven to 375 degrees F. Using an electric mixer, cream the butter, egg, and vanilla. Add the cookie mix. Stir until well blended. Drop the cookies by rounded tablespoonfuls on ungreased cookie sheets. Bake 8 to 10 minutes, until golden brown. Transfer to a wire rack to cool. ❏

Best-Ever Cookie Mix

Makes 6 cups.

1 cup brown sugar
1/2 cup fine granulated sugar
2-1/2 cups flour
1 teaspoon baking soda
1 teaspoon salt
1 cup chopped pecans or walnuts
1 cup mini candy-coated chocolate pieces (such
*   as mini M&Ms)*

Sift together the flour with the baking soda and salt. Layer the flour mixture, sugars, and candies in a glass jar. ❏

These bread mixes are easy to make and easy to bake – a winning combination.

RECIPE

Herb Beer Bread Mix

Makes 2-1/2 cups.

2-2/3 cups flour
2 tablespoons sugar
2 tablespoons baking powder
1 teaspoon salt
1 teaspoon dried oregano
1 teaspoon dried thyme
1/2 teaspoon dried dill

Blend ingredients. Place in a jar. If you like, include a can of beer. ❑

Herb Beer Bread

Makes 1 loaf.

1 jar Herb Beer Bread Mix
A 12 oz. can of beer (or sparkling water)
1/4 cup melted butter

Grease a loaf pan. Preheat the oven to 375 degree F. In a large bowl, combine the Herb Beer Bread Mix with the can of beer or sparkling water. Stir until just moist. Place the batter in the prepared pan. Bake for 45 to 50 minutes. Remove from the oven and brush with melted butter. ❑

Chocolate-dipped Pretzels, Nuts & Dried Fruit Recipe

Making chocolate-dipped treats is a very easy, fun activity for the whole family. Make the production of these tasty treats a holiday tradition in your home.

Dipping Tips:
• Use baking chocolate or chocolate bars – the best chocolate your budget will allow. Using good-quality chocolate (such as Belgian chocolate) makes all the difference in the finished product!
• Do not get any water in the chocolate.
• Do not store finished dipped products in the refrigerator. Store in an airtight jar.

Two Methods for Melting Chocolate
Method #1: Place broken pieces of chocolate over bowl of boiling water. Stir until smooth.
Method #2: Place chocolate in a glass or ceramic dish. Melt in microwave in 15-second intervals, mixing between each.

Items to Dip in Chocolate
Toasted hazelnuts, almonds, or walnuts
Dried raisins, cranberries, or blueberries (pretty with white chocolate)
Dried apricots or papaya spears (pretty with white chocolate)
Candied popcorn
Mini pretzels (Add colorful candy sprinkles before chocolate sets up)

Decorated lids make these jars festive, and the clear glass makes it easy to see the treats inside. Recipes for some yummy treats are on the previous pages or add your own favorite treat to fill these jars.

Christmas Goodies Jars

LARGE JAR

Contents: White chocolate covered pretzels

JAR TYPE

Old-fashioned pint-sized canning jar with wire clamp top

LID DECORATION

1. Cut out paper labels with decorative-edge scissors.
2. Decorate labels with decorative rub-on transfers.
3. Adhere labels to lid.

EMBELLISHMENTS

1. Tie a gold ribbon bow around the neck of the jar.
2. Make a paper gift tag to coordinate with the lid label. Decorate with transfers. ❏

SMALL JAR

Contents: Chocolate covered hazelnuts

JAR TYPE

Small round recycled jar with metal lid

LID DECORATION

1. Cut out paper labels with decorative-edge scissors.
2. Decorate labels with rub-on transfers.
3. Cut a piece of fabric to fit over top of jar. Affix labels to fabric with spray adhesive. Use red elastic cord to secure fabric on lid.

EMBELLISHMENTS

1. Tie a bow of thin gold ribbon around the neck of the jar.
2. Add a paper gift tag to match the lid label. Decorate with transfers. ❏

Pictured right: Snowman Jar, Christmas Goodies Jar.

The best gifts are tied with heartstrings

For each cup of hot cocoa to warm you up add ⅓ cup of cocoa mix to 1 cup boiling water-mix with a cinnamon mm

CHRISTMAS JOY

This jolly snowman can hold a homemade hot chocolate mix or be used to store miniature marshmallows. The recipe is on the following page.

Snowman Jar *pictured on page 93*

RECIPE

Hot Cocoa Mix

Makes 5-1/2 cups

3 cups powdered milk
One 5-oz. package non-instant
  chocolate pudding mix
1/2 cup powdered non-dairy
  creamer
1/4 cup unsweetened cocoa
  powder
1/4 cup icing sugar

Layer ingredients in a quart-sized canning jar. Stir contents before measuring for use.

Cup of Cocoa

Makes 1 cup of cocoa

Stir contents of jar before measuring mix.

Add 1 heaping tablespoon of cocoa mix to 1 cup of boiling water. Stir and enjoy!

Contents: Hot Cocoa Mix (See the "Drink Mixes" section.)

JAR TYPE

Quart-size canning jar with two-piece lid (flat seal and band)

JAR DECORATION

1. Write instructions for making a cup of cocoa on the front of the jar with a black paint pen. ("For a cup of hot cocoa to warm you up, add 1/3 cup of Cocoa Mix to 1 cup boiling water – mix with a cinnamon stick. Mmmmm good!")

2. Glue miniature knitted mittens in place – one holding cinnamon sticks for stirring the cocoa.

LID DECORATION

1. Cut a small section off a 3" diameter plastic foam ball so it will lie flat on the lid. Glue foam ball to lid.

2. Form coal eyes and mouth and carrot nose from polymer clay. Bake according to manufacturer's instructions. Let cool. Paint with acrylic craft paint.

3. Cover the ball head with snow texture paint. Place snowflake sequins in wet paint and position eyes, mouth, and nose in wet snow texture paint. Let dry.

4. Cut a scarf from green felt and wrap around rim. Cut ends to resemble fringe.

5. Decorate scarf and head with snowflake sequins.

6. Highlight eyes and blush cheeks with acrylic craft paints. ❑

Try these drink mixes for filling winter gift jars.

RECIPE
Chai Spice Mix

This makes a warming, spicy cup of tea. It takes a bit more effort to prepare but is well worth the effort. A jar of chai spices is an excellent present for the more adventurous people on your gift list. Tie a small tea strainer (sieve) to the jar to add to the presentation.

Dried ginger pieces
Black peppercorns
Cinnamon sticks, broken into small pieces
Whole cardamom pods
Whole cloves
Whole coriander seed pods

Layer ingredients in equal portions in a jar.

RECIPE
Mulled Cranberry Drink Mix

Makes 1-1/2 cups.

10 cinnamon sticks, broken
1/3 cup whole cloves
1/3 cup whole allspice
2 tablespoons dried orange peel
1/2 cup dried cranberries

Combine all ingredients. Package 1/4 cup of the mix in a piece of cheesecloth and tie with kitchen twine. Fill a jar with cheesecloth packages of drink mix. Tie a 3" cinnamon stick to the top of the bag for a festive presentation. ❑

Authentic Indian Chai Tea

Makes 3 cups.

Chai Spice Mix
Black tea
Whole milk (or soy or rice milk)
Sugar

Mix the Chai Spice Mix. Measure 1 heaping tablespoon Chai Spice Mix and place in a saucepan with 3 cups water. Simmer for 10 minutes. Remove from heat. Add 1 heaping tablespoon black tea. Let steep 5 minutes.

While the tea is steeping, warm 1 cup whole milk until steaming but not boiling. Strain the tea and spice mixture through a sieve. Sweeten to taste with sugar. ❑

Mulled Spiced Cranberry Cider

Makes 2 quarts.

1 package (1/4 cup) Mulled Cranberry Drink Mix
1 quart apple cider
1 quart water
2 fresh oranges, sliced
1/2 pint dark rum

In a large saucepan, combine the cider, water, and Mulled Cranberry Drink Mix. Heat well, but do not boil. Add the orange slices. Serve warm, garnished with an orange slice. ❑

A simple padded fabric top makes this country-style gift a bit more special. What's inside is unique and delicious.

Country Cake-in-a-Jar

Contents: Baked Cake-in-a-Jar (See following pages for recipes.)

JAR TYPE
Pint-size wide-mouth canning jar with two-part lid (flat seal and screw-on band)

LID DECORATION
1. Cut a 7" circle from print or gingham fabric, using pinking shears.
2. Cut a 3" circle of 1/2" thick polyester batting.
3. Center batting circle under fabric circle. Sew a large (1-1/4") button in center of fabric circle and batting.
4. When cake is baked and sealed and jar is cool, place fabric cover over seal and screw on ring.
5. Glue tea-stained lace around band.

EMBELLISHMENTS
1. Make a gift tag of colored paper, 2" x 2-1/2", with a 1-1/2" x 2" panel. Add stickers or transfers with cooking theme motifs. With a gold gel pen, write "Life is short...Eat dessert first" around the edge.
2. Add a wooden spoon, attached with elastic cord. ❑

Cake-in-a-Jar
Cake-in-a-Jar is a baked, ready-to-eat cake that is stored and baked in its container – the jar! (Basically, you are canning a cake.) The cakes last several months without refrigeration and are fun to give as gifts.

Wide-mouth pint-size canning jars with two-part lids (seal and band) are best for Cake-in-a-Jar – the cake can slide easily out after the jar is opened. I also use standard-mouth jars and offer the cakes with a spoon so the cake can be eaten right from the jar.

Follow these steps for successful cakes-in-a-jar every time:

1. Sterilize jars and seals. (You must use new seals.) Let the jars dry.

2. Grease the bottoms and sides of the jars well with butter. Do not use spray oils to grease the jars.

3. Place 1 cup of batter in each jar. Don't use more – if you do, the cake could overflow the jar as it rises.

4. Wipe the tops of the jars well with a clean, damp paper towel. The jar tops need to be clean; if they are not, you will not get a tight seal.

5. Place the jars on a baking sheet, making sure the jars don't touch each other. Bake at 325 degrees F. for 55-60 minutes. Check if the cake is done by inserting a wooden skewer. The cake is cooked when the skewer comes out clean.

6. The jars are very hot after baking. Remove with care, using oven mitts on both hands.

7. Place seals on jars right after the cakes are removed from the oven. Screw on bands firmly, but not too tight. Let cool completely.

8. Check to see that jars have sealed properly. Cakes in jars that do not seal properly can be enjoyed by your family or frozen. Use two months from baking as the "best before" date. If keeping longer, store the cakes in the refrigerator.

RECIPE

Basic Cake-in-a-Jar
Makes 6 to 7 cakes

2-2/3 cup sugar
1 cup butter
4 eggs
1/2 cup water
2 teaspoons vanilla
3-1/2 cups flour
1 teaspoon baking powder
1-1/2 teaspoons baking soda
1 teaspoon salt

Cream sugar and butter. Add eggs and mix well. Add water and vanilla. Add dry ingredients. Pour 1 cup batter in each pint jar. Bake at 325 degrees F. for 55 to 60 minutes.

Cake-in-a-Jar Recipes

This batter is a bit thicker than regular cake batter, and the finished cakes are a little more dense. Don't be afraid to experiment with the basic recipe, or adjust your favorite cake recipes to make in jars. Each recipe makes 6 to 7 jar cakes.

Banana Nut Cake
To Basic Cake-in-a-Jar Recipe, add:

2 cups mashed bananas
1 teaspoon cinnamon
2/3 cup chopped pecans

Mix and bake according to instructions for Basic Cake-in-a-Jar Recipe. ❑

Chocolate Almond Cake

Omit water and vanilla from Basic Cake-in-a-Jar Recipe and add:

1/2 cup almond-flavored liqueur
2 cups semi-sweet chocolate pieces
1 cup almonds

Mix and bake according to instructions for Basic Cake-in-a-Jar Recipe. ❏

Rum Raisin Cake

Omit water from Basic Cake-in-a-Jar Recipe and add:

1/2 cup dark rum
1 cup raisins

Mix and bake according to instructions for Basic Cake-in-a-Jar Recipe. ❏

Polka-Dot Cake Recipe

To Basic Cake-in-a-Jar Recipe, add:

1 cup mini candy-coated
    chocolate candies
    (M&Ms)

Mix and bake according to instructions for Basic Cake-in-a-Jar Recipe. ❏

Orange Poppy Seed Cake

Omit water from Basic Cake-in-a-Jar Recipe and add:

1 cup white chocolate pieces
1/4 cup poppy seeds
1 Tablespoon fresh grated orange rind
1/2 cup orange juice

Mix and bake according to instructions for Basic Cake-in-a-Jar Recipe. ❏

It's easy to create a themed culinary gift basket by using coordinating jar decorations for a collection of jars. Here, red bandanna-print fabric and cowboy-themed stencils and buttons decorate a trio of jars that hold soup mix, cornbread mix, and a mix for dressing or dip. Recipes for these contents are included on the following pages.

Gifts for a Cowboy

Trail Bean Soup Jar

JAR TYPE

Quart-size canning jar with two-part lid

LID DECORATION

1. Cut a 7" circle from red bandanna-print fabric.

2. Place over lid. Wrap gold rope around neck of jar and tie to secure fabric.

3. Glue plastic cowboy-themed button on top.

EMBELLISHMENTS

1. To make the gift tag, stencil a 2" square panel of tan paper with cowboy boots or a cowboy hat. Ink a barbed wire border with a black pen. Cut a 2-1/2" x 5" card and fold. Glue panel to front of card.

2. Add a laminated soup recipe card with stenciled accents.

3. *Optional:* Tie a small bottle of hot sauce to the jar. ❏

Ranch Dressing Jar

JAR TYPE

6 oz. old-fashioned glass canning jar with glass lid and wire clamp

JAR DECORATION

Wrap gold rope around neck of jar.

EMBELLISHMENTS

Print the recipe for Ranch Dressing or Ranch Dip (or both) on card stock. Laminate. Decorate recipe card(s) with a plastic boot button strung on gold elastic cord. ❏

Cowboy Cornbread Jar

JAR TYPE

Pint-size old-fashioned canning jar with glass lid and wire clamp

JAR DECORATION

1. Fold a 10" square red bandanna in half to form a triangle.

2. Tie around neck of jar.

EMBELLISHMENTS

Print recipe on card. Laminate. Accent with stenciled cowboy-themed designs. ❏

RECIPE

Trail Bean Soup Mix

Makes enough to fill a quart-size jar.

1/2 cup pearl barley
1/2 cup red beans
1/2 cup baby lima beans
1/2 cup split peas
1/2 cup pinto beans
1/2 cup blackeyed peas
1/2 cup yellow split peas
1/2 cup navy beans
1/2 cup green or brown lentils

Layer the ingredients in a quart jar. ❑

Turkey Noodle Soup

2 tablespoons vegetable oil
1 medium onion, chopped
3 carrots, peeled and chopped
3 stalks celery, chopped
1 jar Lentil Noodle Soup Mix
8 cups water
2 cups cooked turkey or a smoked turkey leg

Heat the oil in a large stockpot. Add the onion, carrots, and celery. Saute until the vegetables are tender. Add the Lentil Noodle Soup Mix and the water and bring to a boil. Reduce to a simmer. Add cooked turkey and simmer until noodles and lentils are done. ❑

Trail Bean Soup

1 jar Trail Bean Soup Mix
2 quarts water
1 ham hock
1-1/4 teaspoons salt
1 teaspoon pepper
1 can (28 oz.) diced tomatoes
1 large onion, chopped
1 garlic glove, minced

Place bean soup mix in a bowl. Add 2 quarts water and soak overnight. Drain. Bring 2 quarts water and to boil in a soup pot. Add ham hock and simmer 20 minutes. Remove ham hock. Add drained, soaked bean soup mix and remaining ingredients. Bring to boil, reduce heat, and simmer 1 hour. ❑

RECIPE

Lentil Noodle Soup Mix

1/4 cup red lentils
2 tablespoons dried minced onion
1-1/2 tablespoons chicken bouillon granules
1/2 teaspoon dill
1/8 teaspoon celery seed
1/8 teaspoon garlic powder
1 bay leaf
1 cup uncooked egg noodles

Place ingredients in a jar. ❑

RECIPE

Cowboy Cornbread Mix

Makes just over 3 cups.

1 cup flour
2 cups yellow cornmeal
1/3 cup sugar
4 teaspoons baking powder
1 teaspoon salt

Layer in a pint-size canning jar. ❏

Cowboy Cornbread

1 jar Cornbread Mix
1 egg
1 cup milk
1/3 cup melted butter

Preheat oven to 400 degrees F. Blend mix in a large bowl. Mix egg, milk, and butter and add to dry mixture. Stir only until moistened. Pour into greased loaf pan or muffin tin and bake 20-25 minutes. Serve hot with butter. ❏

RECIPE

Ranch Dressing Mix

Makes 1/4 cup.

1-1/2 tablespoons dried parsley
1 tablespoon salt
1/2 tablespoon dried chives
1/4 tablespoon dried oregano
1/4 tablespoon dried tarragon
1/2 tablespoon garlic powder
1/2 tablespoon lemon pepper

Blend all ingredients and package in a small jar. ❏

Ranch Dip

Makes 2 cups.

2 tablespoons Ranch Dressing Mix
1 cup mayonnaise
1 cup sour cream

Combine all ingredients in a bowl. Refrigerate for 2 hours. Serve as a dip for raw vegetables or as a topping for baked potatoes. ❏

Ranch Dressing

Makes 1 cup.

1 tablespoon Ranch Dressing Mix
1/2 cup mayonnaise
1/2 cup buttermilk

Whisk all ingredients together in a bowl. Refrigerate for 1 hour before serving. ❏

These jars are decoupaged with Italian-themed printed napkins. The wooden tops are decorated with polymer clay and painted for a faux antique ivory appearance.

Italian Countryside Jars

Contents: Drink mixes (See the following recipe section.)

JAR TYPE

Glass decorative jars with wooden tops

JAR DECORATION

1. Separate plys of napkins and cut to fit jar.

2. Brush glass paint medium on jar. Arrange napkins over paint medium. Carefully brush over the napkins with a coat of paint medium. (The napkins will wrinkle slightly. Let them – that's part of the look.) Let dry.

3. Wrap moss green colored ribbon around the neck of jar.

4. Tie and secure ends by gluing on an embossed pewter motif.

LID DECORATION

Decorate the lids with faux carved ivory. See "The Faux Carved Ivory Technique" in the section on "Decorating with Polymer Clay."

Tuscan Market Jar

Contents: Tuscan Market Soup Mix (See following pages for recipe.)

JAR TYPE

Large rounded decorative glass jar with wooden lid

JAR DECORATION

1. Wrap an ochre ribbon around neck of jar.

2. Tie and secure ends with embossed pewter motif.

LID DECORATION

Decorate the lid with faux carved ivory. See "The Faux Carved Ivory Technique" in the section on "Decorating with Polymer Clay."

EMBELLISHMENTS

1. Print recipe on a card 3-1/4" square and laminate.

2. Cut a piece of tan card stock 4" x 8". Add a 3-1/2" square rust panel with decoratively cut corners.

3. Slip recipe card in corners of panel. ❑

Pictured at right, left to right: Italian Countryside Jar, Tuscan Market Jar

Tuscan Market Soup

1 Jar Tuscan market Soup Mix
2 stalks Celery
2 sliced Carrots
1 cup shredded cabbage
1 can crushed tomatoes

Add contents . . . ar to 3 quarts water and the
vegetables. Over med. hi . . . cover and simmer
1 hour until vegetables tender.

L'olio d'oliva cura tutti

Herb blends are easy and inexpensive to make. They are appropriate gifts for all cooks and are excellent for people on salt-restricted diets. If you use herbs harvested from your garden, make sure they are absolutely dry. If they're not, the blend could get moldy.

Mediterranean Herbs Jar

Contents: Mediterranean Herb Blend, Lemon Dill Herb Blend, Herbes de Provence (See following pages for recipes.)

JAR TYPE

Small glass canning jar with glass top and wire clamp

JAR DECORATION

Wrap a gold ribbon around the neck of jar and tie. Glue an embossed pewter motif over the ends of the ribbon.

LID DECORATION

Decorate the lid with faux carved ivory. See "The Faux Carved Ivory Technique" in the section on "Decorating with Polymer Clay."

EMBELLISHMENTS

Include laminated recipe cards with printed with recipes for using the herb blend. ❑

RECIPE

Mediterranean Herb Blend Recipe

Makes 3/4 cup.

3 tablespoons sun-dried
   tomatoes
2 tablespoons dried basil
2 tablespoons dried parsley
1 tablespoon dried oregano
1/2 tablespoon dried garlic
   granules
1/2 tablespoon dried lemon peel
1 teaspoon dried red pepper
   flakes

Blend all ingredients. Place in a cellophane bag or a small jar. ❑

Pictured at right, left to right: Villa Biscotti Jar, Mediterranean Herbs Jar, Italian Countryside Jar

Mediterranean Vinaigrette

1 tablespoon Mediterranean Herb Blend
¼ cup olive oil
Juice of one lemon
1 tablespoon sugar

Mix all the ingredients and refrigerate for a few hours
the flavors to blend. Mix well before pouring on
vegetables.

The lid of this jar is decorated with a decoupaged paper napkin and a polymer clay banner.

Villa Biscotti Jar

Pictured on page 107

JAR TYPE

Glass cookie jar with wooden lid

JAR DECORATION

1. Tie a light tan grosgrain ribbon around the neck of the jar.
2. Accent with a silk olive branch.

LID DECORATION

1. Decoupage a paper napkin printed with an Italian scene on the lid.
2. Make a banner from polymer clay. Stamp "Villa Biscotti" on the banner, using alphabet rubber stamps. Bake according to clay manufacturer's instructions. Let cool. Paint banner with ivory acrylic craft paint. Paint lettering with dark brown acrylic craft paint.
3. Glue banner to lid. Add a grape cluster charm and a wine bottle charm. ❏

Use these recipes to fill your jars with European flavor.

RECIPE

Tuscan Market Soup Mix

1/2 cup barley
1/2 cup split peas
1/2 cup rice
1/2 cup lentils
2 tablespoons dried minced onion
2 tablespoons dried parsley
2 teaspoons salt
1/2 teaspoon pepper
2 tablespoons beef bouillon granules
1 teaspoon dried cumin
1 pkg. dehydrated onion soup mix

Layer ingredients in a quart jar. ❏

Tuscan Market Soup

1 jar Tuscan Market Soup Mix
3 quarts water
2 stalks celery, chopped
2 carrots, sliced
1 cup shredded cabbage
1 can (28 oz.) crushed tomatoes

Combine ingredients and place in soup pot. Cover. Cook over medium heat and simmer 1 hour, until vegetables are tender. ❏

Mediterranean Herb Vinaigrette

1 tablespoon Mediterranean Herb Blend
1/4 cup olive oil
Juice of one lemon

Mix all ingredients. Refrigerate for a few hours to allow the flavors to blend. Stir to mix well before pouring on salad greens or grilled vegetables. ❑

RECIPE

Lemon Dill Herb Blend

Makes 1/2 cup.

4 tablespoons dried parsley
2 tablespoons dried dill
1 tablespoon dried lemon peel
1 tablespoon dried garlic granules

Blend all ingredients and place in a small jar. ❑

RECIPE

Herbes de Provence Recipe

Makes 1/2 cup.

2 tablespoons marjoram
2 tablespoons dried oregano
1 tablespoon dried rosemary
1 tablespoon dried thyme
2 teaspoons dried lavender buds
2 teaspoons dried fennel seeds

Blend ingredients and place in a small jar. ❑

Grilled Lemon Dill Chicken

Serves 6.

1 tablespoon Lemon Dill Herb Blend
1/4 cup olive oil
1/4 cup fresh lemon juice
6 chicken breasts

In a shallow dish, stir together Lemon Dill Herb Blend, lemon juice, and oil. Add the chicken breasts and marinate in the refrigerator for 1 hour. Grill over hot coals or under the broiler until done. ❑

French Country Fried Fish

Serves 4.

1 tablespoon Herbes de Provence
2 cups dried bread crumbs
1 egg, beaten
1 pound white fish fillets (halibut, cod, or haddock)
1 tablespoon vegetable oil

Mix the herb blend and the crumbs on wax paper. Dip the fish pieces in egg, then in the crumb mixture. Shake off excess. Heat the oil in a pan and fry the fish until golden and the fish flakes easily with a fork. ❑

A purchased stencil makes this a quickie project. Filled with homemade doggy biscuits, it's a great bazaar item – who can resist a gift for the canine member of the family?

Stenciled Doggy Treats Jar

Baked Doggy Treats Recipe

1 pint-size jar Doggy Treats mix
1/4 cup water
1 egg

1. Mix all ingredients in a bowl. Turn out on a board.
2. Knead into dough. Roll out and cut out shapes.
3. Bake for 30 minutes in a 400 oven, then turn down oven to 200 degrees. Leave biscuits to dry slowly in oven until bone hard. ❑

JAR TYPE

Square decorative glass jar with glass-and-wire lid

JAR DECORATION

1. Stencil "woof" and dog prints on the front of the jar. Use green enamel glass paint for the lettering and brown for the paw prints. Let dry.
2. Outline letters with a gold paint pen.
3. Glue plastic dog buttons with the shanks removed on the front of the jar.

LID DECORATION

1. Stencil a large heart on the top of the lid using red enamel paint forglass. Let dry.
2. Remove shanks from dog and bone buttons, if they have them. Glue on lid.

EMBELLISHMENTS

1. Buckle an old dog collar around the neck of the jar.
2. Make a layered paper tag. Glue a dog button, shank removed, in the center of the tag.
3. Punch a hole in the tag and attach to the jar with gold cord. ❑

Doggy Treats Mix Jar

Contents: Doggy Treats Mix (layer the ingredients in the jar)

JAR TYPE

Pint-size canning jar

LID DECORATION

Paper circle cut from green decorative paper, square panels in the middle with dog and heart stickers.

EMBELLISHMENTS

1. Make a recipe card with the baking instructions (the Baked Doggy Treats Recipe). Accent with doggy stickers and laminate.
2. Make a tag by folding a 2-1/2" x 5" piece of paper. Decorate front with squares of decorative paper panels (2"and 1"). Accent with ball, dog, and heart stickers. ❑

RECIPE

Doggy Treats Mix

Use this mix and the recipe above to make Baked Doggy Treats. This amount will fill a pint jar.

1 cup whole wheat flour
1/2 cup powdered milk
1/2 cup soy bacon bits
1 teaspoon sea salt
1/8 cup sugar
1 tablespoon beef bouillon granules or powder

Layer the mix in the jar. ❑

Doggy Treats
1 jar Doggy Treats Mix
¼ cup water
1 egg

Blend all ingredients in a bowl mix well. Turn out onto a floured board and knead into soft dough. Roll out to ¼" thick, use a cookie cutter and cut out treats. Place on un-greased cookie sheet and bake in a 400 oven for 50 minuets. Turn oven down to 200 and leave biscuits to dry slowly until bone hard.

Homemade fragrance gifts are pampering and a delight to receive. The decorated jars can be displayed in the bath or bedroom.

GIFTS OF SCENT

You can buy a gel air freshener base at crafts stores that you can use to create sparkling, scented gifts in a jar. The gel base is odorless and colorless; you simply melt it in a microwave oven and add scents and colors of your choosing.

The air freshener, packaged in a glass jar with a metal screw-on top with holes, works like this: As the scented gel dehydrates, it releases its fragrance. (It also gets smaller – to rehydrate to the original size, simply add a small amount of distilled water.) Jars that contain gel air fresheners are the Floral Fragrance Jar (instructions on page 46), Joyful Scents Jar, French Country Air Jar, and Magical Scents Jar.

Making Gel Air Fresheners

Because the air freshener gel is completely water-soluble, it's important to use water-based colorants and water-based fragrances made especially for coloring and scenting it. Other fragrances, such as perfumes and essential oils, will make the gel look cloudy.

Note: There are many recipes for gel air fresheners made with gelatin, but I haven't found one that worked for me. The ones I made myself grew moldy very quickly, and they were always cloudy.

How to Make Gel Air Fresheners

YOU'LL NEED:

Unscented, uncolored air fresher gel base

Water-soluble color tints

Water-soluble fragrance concentrate

Heat-resistant glass measuring cup

HERE'S HOW:

1. Scoop the gel base from the container and place into a heat-resistant glass measuring cup. Place in microwave for 1 minute on medium-high. Continue heating at 15-second intervals until completely melted.

2. Add water-soluble color tints one drop at a time until desired color is achieved.

3. Add water-soluble fragrance concentrate, using up to 1/2 ounce of fragrance concentrate to 8 ounces gel. Stir lightly.

4. Pour scented, colored gel in the jar. Cool until firm. *For a faster set, place container with gel in a pan of cold water.* ❏

Pictured clockwise, from top left: Magical Scents Jar, French Country Air Jar, Joyful Scents Jar, Ocean Breeze Jar, Floral Fragrance Jar (see page 46 for instructions.

This gel air freshener lightly keeps the room refreshed and smelling sweet. The clear purple hue is bright and uplifting – reminiscent of a clear day in the country with fields of lavender.

French Country Air Jar

Contents: Gel air freshener colored with 3 drops blue colorant and 3 drops red colorant (medium purple). Add a pinch of multicolored sparkle powder and 1/2 oz. water-based lavender fragrance.

JAR TYPE

12-oz. recycled glass globe with gold lid

JAR DECORATION

Create a faux etched-glass design, using a small fleur de lis motif stencil and a dense foam applicator with frosted white transparent glass paint. Be sure the paint has dried on one motif before moving on to the next to prevent smudging.

LID DECORATION

Punch a fleur de lis motif on the lid. See instructions below.

EMBELLISHMENTS

1. Wrap a 12" piece of gold cord around the neck of the jar. Tie in a knot.
2. Glue a purple silk orchid and orchid buds to ribbon knot.
3. Loop and glue gold bullion under the flower for a sparkling accent. ❑

Punched Metal Lids

Metal lids with holes are decorative and help distribute the scent from gel air fresheners. You can buy metal lids that already have holes in them or you can make your own punched lids using this simple technique.

YOU'LL NEED:
Jar with a metal screw-on lid
Hammer
Awl
Tracing paper
Low-tack masking tape

HERE'S HOW:
1. Trace the punch design on a piece of paper. Tape the paper to the top of the lid.
2. Place the lid on a firm surface and, using an awl and a hammer, lightly tap in the holes.
   • You can adjust the size of the holes easily – tap harder to make bigger holes.
   • Be careful not to hammer too hard – you could warp the lid. ❑

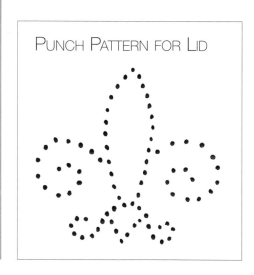

PUNCH PATTERN FOR LID

A simple jar is made extraordinary with a faux etched glass design and faux stained glass accents. The perforated lid, purchased in the gel fragrance section at a crafts store, helps release the clean scent of the fragrance gel.

Joyful Scents Jar

Contents: Gel air freshener base with silver sparkle powder, colored with green colorant, scented with 1/2 oz. juniper fragrance (See "How to Make Gel Air Fresheners.")

Pictured left to right: Joyful Scents Jar, French Country Air Jar

JAR TYPE
Straight-sided 8-oz. glass jar with decoratively perforated gold lid

JAR DECORATION
Create a faux etched glass design, using a "Joy" stencil and a dense foam applicator with frosty white transparent glass paint.

EMBELLISHMENTS
1. Wrap gold metallic ribbon around top of jar. Glue a narrow red satin ribbon with gold edges to gold metallic ribbon.

2. Paint a faux stained glass design on a plastic sheet, using pattern provided. Cut out motifs. Glue with clear silicon glue to the jar. ❏

Clear scented gel is poured over a jar of shells for a charming presentation with the smell of the tropics.

Ocean Breeze Jar *pictured on page 113*

PUNCH PATTERN FOR LID

Contents: Gel air freshener (Fill jar with shells. Add gold sparkle powder and tropical melon fragrance to clear gel base and pour over shells.)

JAR TYPE

6-oz. hexagonal recycled glass jar with gold metal lid

JAR DECORATION

1. Wrap a cream-colored cord around neck of jar and knot.
2. Glue knot to jar and add a small shell.

LID DECORATION

Punch holes in a spiral pattern. See instructions at the beginning of this section.

EMBELLISHMENTS

Emboss a brass metal tag with "Ocean Breeze." Punch with a star punch. Attach with a gold cord. ❑

This sparkling, fresh scented gel air freshener comes in a sparkling jar. For extra sparkle, add bubbles to the jar this way: Before pouring in the scented and colored liquid gel in the jar, fill it about three-quarters full with small pieces of clear air freshener gel base right from the container. These pieces will trap air, creating bubbles.

Magical Scents Jar *pictured on page 113*

Contents: Gel air freshener (Color gel air freshener base with 3 drops yellow and 1 drop red for a bright orange hue. Add a pinch of gold sparkle powder and 1/2 bottle of tangerine water-based fragrance. See "How to Make Gel Air Fresheners.")

JAR TYPE

8-oz straight sided round jar with a gold perforated lid

LID DECORATION

Glue acrylic rhinestones around the top of the perforated lid.

JAR DECORATION

1. String gold beads and gold star buttons on a 20" piece of gold cord. Wrap the jeweled cord around the jar twice.
2. Add some gold bullion, wrapped around the jar, for extra sparkle.
3. Glue acrylic rhinestones around the jar.

EMBELLISHMENTS

To make a tag, cut a 2" x 4" piece of gold paper and fold into a card. Glue a 1-1/2" white paper panel to the card. Punch front of card with a star punch. Glue a gold button (shank removed), gold bullion, and rhinestones to the white panel. Punch the corner of the tag with a star and add a loop of thin gold cord to attach. ❑

More recipe ideas for filling jars with lovely scents.

Holiday Simmer

Simmering potpourris are popular because of their ability to quickly fill the house with fragrance. They are specially formulated to be visually appealing and aromatic.

This simple recipe can be packaged in a small round jar that has been decorated with holiday motifs. (See the Joyful Scents Jar for decorating ideas.) Be sure to include instructions for use.

Layer equal amounts in a jar:
Broken cinnamon sticks
Whole cloves
Dried lemon peel
Dried orange peel

To use: Add 3 tablespoons of the spice blend to 1 quart simmering water in a glass saucepan. Reduce heat and gently simmer on the stove, adding more hot water as needed. Do not let the mixture come to a full boil. Discard the mixture after use. ❑

Layered Potpourri

Glass jars are perfect containers for attractively displaying fragrant collections of dried botanicals. Simply layer the dried botanicals in the jar, packing down after each layer, and add fragrance to the top layer of botanicals. (Additional fragrance can be added as needed — you could include a small bottle of fragrance oils for refreshing with your gift.)

Some of the projects that contain layered potpourri include the Lavender Fields Jar and the Mocha Java Jar. Instructions for these jars can be found on the following pages.

Coffee-scented Layered Potpourri

Layer 1" of each ingredient in a one-quart jar in this order:

Carob bean pods
Natural Milo berries
Coffee beans
Cinnamon sticks in 1" pieces
Natural Milo berries
Coffee beans
Whole allspice berries

Scent with 20 drops chocolate fragrance oil and 20 drops espresso fragrance oil to the top of the jar. Be sure to label "Do not consume." ❑

This beautiful-to-look-at jar is filled with a clean-smelling potpourri. Fill the space between the neck of the jar and the lid with crumpled clear plastic wrap to keep contents from shifting.

Ocean Bouquet Jar

Contents: Layered potpourri (oak moss, whole blue juniper berries, small white clam shells, blue larkspur flowers, white snail shells, oak moss, and twisted leaves in 1" layers, topped with blue larkspur flowers and white snail shells and scented with 20 drops peppermint and 20 drops lavender fragrance oils)

JAR TYPE

8" tall clear glass jar with glass lid and wire clamp closure

JAR DECORATION

1. Tie a net-like natural cotton ribbon around the top of the jar.
2. Glue shells at the knot to accent. Write "Ocean Bouquet" inside one shell with a black permanent marker.

LID DECORATION

1. Glue an arrangement of shells on top of the lid with silicon-based glue.
2. Glue a blue bead in one shell (like a pearl) to accent.

EMBELLISHMENTS

Make a gift tag from a 2" x 4" piece of purple card stock. Fold. Add a 1-1/2" square gray panel and a ship sticker. ❏

This lamp jar recalls a beach vacation. The sand castle in the jar is molded from white polymer clay. The clay was baked, allowed to cool, and painted light gray, then sprinkled with sand while the paint was still wet.

Beachfront Property Lamp

Contents: White coral gravel (from an aquarium shop), white sand, small white shells, a message written on paper and placed in a tiny glass bottle, sandcastle

JAR TYPE

Quart-size glass canning jar with a lid lamp kit

JAR DECORATION

1. Stencil sea motifs, clouds, and shells with frosty white transparent glass paint for a faux etched look.
2. Use rub-on transfers to add words ("hope," "wish," "dream," "believe," "imagine") at sand level.
3. Tie natural raffia around the neck of the jar. Make a tassel with the ends.

EMBELLISHMENTS

1. Emboss a piece of 36-gauge silver metal with the words "Beach Front Property." Antique with white metal paint. Punch with a star-shaped punch and attach with a piece of raffia.
2. Make a gift tag from a 1-1/2" x 2-1/2" piece of tan parchment card stock. Add a 1" x 2-1/4" white panel with beach-themed sticker. Punch with a hole punch and attach. ❏

SPECIAL GIFTS

A simple-to-make gift for a bird lover or gardener.

Picnic for the Birds

Contents: Layered birdseed (hulled and unhulled sunflower seeds, chick corn, millet, thistle, raw peanuts)

JAR TYPE

Quart-size canning jar with two-part lid

LID DECORATION

1. Make a nest to fit on top of lid with a small handful of Spanish moss and thin-bodied white glue. Form and place on wax paper to dry.
2. Paint three 1" long wooden eggs with blue paint. Speckle with dark brown.
3. Wrap green raffia around band and tie in a bow. Glue a small rusty birdhouse shape in the center of the bow.

EMBELLISHMENTS

Make a gift tag from a 2" x 5" piece of moss green card stock. Fold. Cut a 1" x 1-1/2" light blue panel and speckle with dark brown paint. Glue to card. Glue a rusty bird shape to the panel. ❑

A lovely botanical accent for any room – the jar of potpourri gives off a pleasant perfume through its fabric top.

Lavender Fields Jar

Contents: Layered dried botanicals in this order: 1 cup oak moss, 1 cup pink rosebuds, 1 cup rosemary leaves, 1 cup blue juniper berries, 1 cup pink rosebuds, 1 cup French lavender buds, 1 cup rosemary leaves. Fill the remaining space with oak moss that has been scented with 20 drops lavender and 10 drops rose fragrance oils.

JAR TYPE

Quart-size clear canning jar with a screw-on band

LID DECORATION

1. Cut a 5" circle of muslin and stamp with a decorative stamp.
2. Cut a 1/2" thick piece of polyester batting the same size as the muslin.
3. Place the batting under the muslin circle and sew a running stitch 1/4" from the edge. Pull thread tightly to gather around the band, secure with a few stitches, and knot.
4. Cut a 20" piece of 1-1/2" wide silk ribbon and rubber stamp with a small fleur de lis stamp along one edge (this will be the bottom) every 1-1/2".
5. Sew a running stitch 1/2" from top edge of the ribbon using 1/4" stitches. Pull the thread to gather the ribbon. Glue along the edge of the band, hiding the raw edges of the padded muslin top.
6. Cut 30" of gold rope. Tie around the band and knot. Glue a polymer clay seal at the knot.

EMBELLISHMENTS

Cut a 2" x 3" piece of cream paper. Fold to make a card and stamp with a decorative rubber stamp. Punch a hole in the corner of the tag. Add a thin gold cord loop to attach it to the jar. ❑

The raised design on this jar was painted to look like etched glass. Any jar with a similar raised design can be painted with this technique.

Faux Etched Glass Tea Jar

Contents: Loose tea

JAR TYPE

Small decorative embossed jar with glass lid and wire clamp closure

JAR DECORATION

Lightly sponge the raised areas of the jar with frosted white transparent glass paint to create a faux etched glass design.

LID DECORATION

1. Press fresh leaves into pieces of polymer clay to make leaf shapes. Cut out leaves and arrange.
2. Using rubber alphabet stamps, press the word "TEA" in the clay. Bake according to manufacturer's instructions.
3. Paint with acrylic craft paints. Let dry.
4. Glue tea leaves and a small teacup on the lid.
5. Apply a resin coating, following the instructions in the section titled "Making Resin-coated Jars & Lids."

EMBELLISHMENTS

Hook a metal tea ball to the wire clamp. ❏

Mocha Java Candle Jar

Contents: Coffee-scented Layered Potpourri. *See page 127 for layering instructions.*

JAR TYPE

Quart-size canning jar fitted with a votive candle holder

JAR DECORATION

1. Cut a piece of 36 gauge copper 10" x 1-1/2". Turn long edges under 1/4" and press flat.
2. With a ballpoint pen, emboss "Wake up and smell the coffee."
3. Wrap band around neck of jar.
4. Affix an antique coffee label to the front of the jar. This can be decoupaged or made into a sticker.

LID DECORATION

1. Place a clear glass flowerpot-shaped votive candleholder inside jar opening. (Choose one that fits your jar.)
2. Place a cream-colored votive candle in the candleholder. Sprinkle a few coffee beans around the candle.

Pictured at right, clockwise from top: Mocha Java Candle Jar, Faux Etched Glass Tea Jar, Is It Coffee Yet? Jar. See instructions for Is It Coffee Yet on page 64.

Cup of
Cappuccino

Stir contents of jar before
measuring.
Measure 2 tablespoons mix
into blender. Add 1 cup boiling water. Process until
foamy. Use
Sprinkle with nutmeg. Use
cinnamon sticks to stir.

HOLIDAY DELIGHTS

Beautiful and fragrant, this jar makes a lovely holiday gift. The lid decoration is removable and can be used as an ornament.

Seasonal Scents

Contents: Layered potpourri (Fill the jar with these items in this order: 1" preserved cedar tips, 1" of 1" cinnamon stick pieces, 7-8 gold cedar roses arranged in a circle around jar, 1" whole rose hips, 1" preserved cedar tips, 1" cranberry eucalyptus bells. Fill to top with whole star anise. Add 20 drops cinnamon orange fragrance oil and 20 drops rose fragrance oil.)

JAR TYPE

5-1/2" tall old-fashioned canning jar with glass lid and bail

JAR DECORATION

1. Cut 16" of 3/8" wide gold ribbon. Tie around neck of jar.
2. Add a gold angel charm and a bit of gold bullion.

LID DECORATION

1. Cut 20" thin gold ribbon. Make a 2" loop on one side of a 2-1/2" wooden disc. Let the ends trail across the disc.
2. Glue an 8" long piece of gold ribbon around the edge of the wooden disc.
3. Glue preserved cedar tips, gold-painted cedar rose, two dried red roses, small pine cones, whole star anise, and a gold angel charm on disc. Accent with gold bullion.
4. Place ornament on top of the jar. Place the loop over the wire clamp. Tie the ribbon ends in a bow to the wire hinge.

EMBELLISHMENTS

To make a gift card, cut a 3" x 6" piece of dark red card stock. Fold. Add a 2-1/2" square gold panel. Glue on a gold plastic snowflake. ❏

This jar holds a collection of inspirational words on small Christmas ornaments. About 16 to 18 ball ornaments (1" and 1-1/2" in diameter). Inspirational words could include "joy," "peace," "Noel," "faith," "inspire," "cheer," "magic," "kiss," "hug," "wish," "believe," "celebrate," "cheer," and "love." You could also use names, special dates, and special occasions. Present it with a small live tree or rosemary bush trimmed with tiny white lights.

Christmas Cheer

Contents: Ball ornaments with words of inspiration written on them with a maroon paint pen and maroon ribbon tied on bows around necks

JAR TYPE

Glass recycled jar, 4.5" tall, with cork top to fit opening

Christmas Cheer (cont.)

JAR DECORATION

1. Tie a bow with maroon ribbon around neck of jar.
2. Add a silver heart charm and silver bullion.

LID DECORATION

1. Cover top and top edge of cork with silk pine rope.
2. Write inspirational words on 4 ball ornaments with a paint pen.

3. Trim with silver heart charms, maroon ribbon bow, and silver bullion. ❑

Pictured above: Christmas Cheer, Light of My Life, Seasonal Scents. See instructions for Light of My Life on page 44.

RECIPE

Favorite Blend Tea Mix

Makes 1/3 cup.

1 teaspoon lemon verbena leaves
1 teaspoon dried peppermint leaves
1 teaspoon rose hips
1-teaspoon hibiscus flowers
3 tablespoons orange pekoe tea

Combine ingredients and package in a small jar. ❏

A Perfect Pot of Tea

Makes 1 pot of tea.

Warm a 6-cup teapot with a cup of boiling water. Discard the water. Place the contents of the package of tea mix (1/3 cup) in the teapot. Heat water in a kettle and, when at a full boil, pour over the tea mix. Let steep for 3 minutes for weak tea and no longer than 6 minutes for strong tea.

Serve with cream, sugar, or lemon, if desired. ❏

RECIPE

Candied Ginger Scone Mix

This is not an attractive mix, so it's best presented in an opaque, painted jar. The recipe makes 6 cups.

3 cups all purpose flour
1 cup buttermilk powder
1-1/2 tablespoon baking powder
1/2 tablespoon cream of tartar
3/4 cup brown sugar
1 teaspoon salt
1/2 cup shortening
1/2 cup candied ginger, finely chopped

Sift the dry ingredients together. Cut in the shortening with a pastry cutter until the mixture resembles fine crumbs. Add the candied ginger. Divide into 2-cup portions. Package each portion in a pint-size jar. ❏

Candied Ginger Scones

Makes 12 scones.

2 cups (1 jar) Candied Ginger Scone Mix
1 egg
1/3 cup light cream

Preheat the oven to 400 degrees F. Place the scone mix in a large bowl. Lightly beat the egg and add to the mix. Add the cream and stir until mixture forms a ball. Be careful not to over mix.

Turn the dough out on a lightly floured surface and pat to a 3/4" thickness. Cut the dough in 12 pieces of equal size. Arrange 2" apart on an ungreased baking sheet. Bake for 10 to 15 minutes until lightly browned. ❏

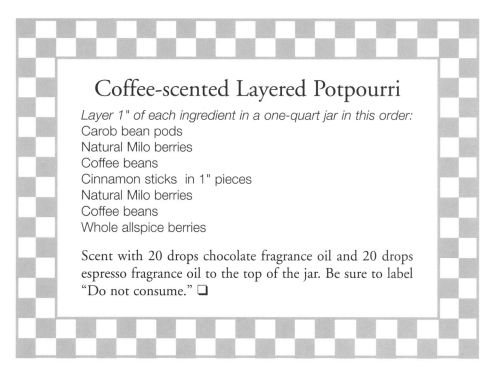

Coffee-scented Layered Potpourri

Layer 1" of each ingredient in a one-quart jar in this order:
Carob bean pods
Natural Milo berries
Coffee beans
Cinnamon sticks in 1" pieces
Natural Milo berries
Coffee beans
Whole allspice berries

Scent with 20 drops chocolate fragrance oil and 20 drops espresso fragrance oil to the top of the jar. Be sure to label "Do not consume." ❑

Metric Conversion Chart

INCHES TO MILLIMETERS AND CENTIMETERS

Inches	MM	CM		Yards	Meters
1/8	3	.3		1/8	.11
1/4	6	.6		1/4	.23
3/8	10	1.0		3/8	.34
1/2	13	1.3		1/2	.46
5/8	16	1.6		5/8	.57
3/4	19	1.9		3/4	.69
7/8	22	2.2		7/8	.80
1	25	2.5		1	.91
1-1/4	32	3.2		2	1.83
1-1/2	38	3.8		3	2.74
1-3/4	44	4.4		4	3.66
2	51	5.1		5	4.57
3	76	7.6		6	5.49
4	102	10.2		7	6.40
5	127	12.7		8	7.32
6	152	15.2		9	8.23
7	178	17.8		10	9.14
8	203	20.3			
9	229	22.9			
10	254	25.4			
11	279	27.9			
12	305	30.5			

Index